Design-Inspired
INNOVATION

Dear Tim,

Your ideas have been a
major influence on this project
and my work in general.

with my appreciation.

J. Utterback

April 2007

# Design-Inspired INNOVATION

James Utterback (MIT, USA)

Bengt-Arne Vedin (Mälardalen University, Sweden)

Eduardo Alvarez (VIGIX, Inc.)

Sten Ekman (Mälardalen University, Sweden)

Susan Walsh Sanderson (Rensselaer Polytechnic Institute, USA)

Bruce Tether (University of Manchester, UK)

Roberto Verganti (Politecnico di Milano, Italy)

**World Scientific**

NEW JERSEY · LONDON · SINGAPORE · BEIJING · SHANGHAI · HONG KONG · TAIPEI · CHENNAI

*Published by*

World Scientific Publishing Co. Pte. Ltd.

5 Toh Tuck Link, Singapore 596224

*USA office:* 27 Warren Street, Suite 401-402, Hackensack, NJ 07601

*UK office:* 57 Shelton Street, Covent Garden, London WC2H 9HE

**Library of Congress Cataloging-in-Publication Data**
Utterback, James M., 1941–
   Design-inspired innovation / by James Utterback . . . [et al.]
      p. cm.
   Includes bibliographical references and index.
   ISBN 10 981-256-694-5 (alk. paper) -- ISBN 10 981-256-695-3 (pbk. : alk. paper)
   ISBN 13 978-981-256-694-2 -- ISBN 13 978-981-256-695-9 (pbk)
     1. Design, Industrial. 2. Engineering design--Technological innovations.
   I. Title.

TS171.D465 2007
745.2--dc22

2006049625

**British Library Cataloguing-in-Publication Data**
A catalogue record for this book is available from the British Library.

Inhouse editor: Juliet Lee Ley Chin

Typeset by Stallion Press
Email: enquiries@stallionpress.com

*Printed by Mainland Press Pte Ltd*

# Contents

# *PREFACE*

Our purpose in writing *Design-Inspired Innovation* is to explore the ways in which communities of art, design, and innovation are merging and influencing each other in the world of material culture to create great new products. What makes products great? What is the role of design firms in creativity and innovation, and how is this role changing? What accounts for design firms' successes? How are the processes of innovation and design changing? Does a focus on design inspire innovation and enhance chances of competitive success? What strategies might result in more inspired design and innovation?

This book reports the results of a study undertaken to explore these questions, which included interviews with the founders of nearly 100 design firms in four countries — Sweden, Italy, England, and the United States — and in several industries. The sample ranged from three divisions of the largest international design firm to some of the smallest and newest firms working in their local areas. We have looked broadly at contributions to advancing innovation and design in several types of products, including consumer electronics, devices for personal mobility, and others.

Manufacturers are responding to changes in technology and market demands by trying to introduce new products into the market more rapidly. They struggle with new and converging technologies that create opportunities for developing entire new product categories and with the entry of new types of competitors. Larger firms enjoy great resources in technology and science, but these resources seem to be growing more available and open to all. Smaller groups and organizations derive greater innovative capabilities from the widening variety of sophisticated design resources available, such as computer-aided design, simulation, and visualization techniques.

We conclude that products, to be successful, must be distinguished by more than sufficient function, consistent quality, and low cost. Our findings and examples imply that considerable competitive advantage might be gained by reconsidering traditional products with a fresh eye and approach that employs newer materials and design techniques. Why do only a few of the welter of products on the market seem to account for the bulk of sales and profits in many categories? We believe it is because these products emphasize customer delight, elegance, and enduring value. They may even acquire increasing value over time.

Our work could be said to have begun with a puzzle posed in 1980. Sweden's larger firms were dramatically reducing employment within Sweden while expanding abroad. At the same time, the formation of new firms in Sweden was in marked decline. Where were the growth and jobs to secure the future of the economy to be found? Could a way be found to stimulate the development of new products and new companies and thus secure the future?

Jim Utterback and Bengt-Arne Vedin became part of a team of Swedish and American researchers asked to conduct a study to address sources for future growth. Their working hypothesis was that the creation of new firms based on technological innovation might lead to a net creation of wealth, jobs, and exports. They proceeded to study 60 new firms in Sweden — about half the population of technology-based start-ups founded in the previous 15 years — and a similar number around Boston for comparative purposes.[1]

The American firms matched Jim and Bengt-Arne's expectations, although their export performance was relatively weak. A mere quarter of the Swedish firms, however, were truly based on new technologies as their main competitive advantage. Another quarter identified their advantage as "design." Jim and Bengt-Arne found these firms to be almost the entirety of the sample enjoying rapid growth. Firms lacking advantages in technology or design tended to grow slowly or not at all. If anything, the firms stressing design were the most successful in the sample.

At the time, Jim and Bengt-Arne did not follow up on this provocative idea, but the study was the start of a long friendship and conversation.

Later, Jim and Bengt-Arne met Susan Sanderson, who was pondering a similar puzzle among firms in Japan that produced portable music players. Among the myriad models being offered, only a few lasted more than briefly in the market and those few garnered the lion's share of all sales and profits. Most were produced by one firm, Sony, and seemed again to emphasize design in addition to function. In fact, the name of

Sony's product — the Walkman — became almost the generic name for portable music players.

A sabbatical at the Harvard Business School in the fall of 1997 gave Jim a chance to share an office with Roberto Verganti. Roberto was part of a larger group of researchers investigating the role of designers and design firms in the economic health and growth of Milan and Lombardy. Could excellence in design be a key ingredient in ensuring a vibrant economy?

An invitation to join the advisory board of the Centre for Research on Innovation and Competition (CRIC) at the University of Manchester led Jim to find that Bruce Tether was in the midst of analyzing data from firms that had received the Millennium Design Awards in the United Kingdom. The awards were given for the most notable new products to appear in the country. While many were indeed highly innovative in a technical sense, an even greater source of success seemed to be either the formal or implicit effort toward excellence and balance in design.

When Bengt-Arne joined the Department of Innovation, Design & Product Development at Mälardalen University, headed by Sten Ekman, Jim and he decided that the time was right to act more directly on their hunch that outstanding product design offered an unappreciated means to competitive and economic success. Our first meeting led to an agreement to conduct a parallel study, with each of us working intensively in our own countries. We were joined by a number of students along the way, one of whom, Eduardo Alvarez — a talented designer and entrepreneur — also became a partner in our work. Coordination took the form of two meetings each year rotating among our various universities and at several conferences where preliminary work was presented. Heads of local design firms participated enthusiastically in several of these gatherings, notably in Milan and Sweden.

While we were searching for general themes we were immediately struck by how diverse the environments and ways of working seemed to be in our different countries. These observations have taken root in our discussion of the differing nature of the design systems and networks in each area studied. We also discovered a sharp difference of opinion within our group around which variables and relationships might hold greater sway in creating value. Should excellence in function and cost weigh more heavily, or might people be more attuned to symbols and to the meanings conveyed in their use of various products? The issue of combining balance and wholeness in a user's experience is indeed the crux of the problem. After presenting our evidence, we attempt to answer this question in the final chapter.[2]

**Endnotes**

---

[1] J. M. Utterback, M. Meyer, E. Roberts, and G. Reitberger, 1988.
[2] The range of questions covered in our interviews is provided in Appendix A. In most interviews, we covered only a selection of these questions.

# ACKNOWLEDGMENTS

We appreciate the grantors of funding and assistance that made it possible for us to pursue our work. These include: the David J. McGrath jr Foundation, for funds provided by Jim Utterback's endowed chair at MIT; the MIT Sloan School of Management and MIT's Leaders for Manufacturing Program; the Economic and Social Research Council (ESRC), through its funding of the ESRC Centre for Research on Innovation and Competition (CRIC) at the University of Manchester; ESRC and the Engineering and Physical Sciences Research Council (EPSRC) through the award to Bruce Tether of a Ghoshal Fellowship with the UK's Advanced Institute of Management Research (AIM); the Swedish Agency for Innovation Systems; the Swedish Industrial Design Foundation; the Savings Bank Foundation of Rekarne in Sweden; *Fondo per gli investimenti in ricerca di base* (FIRB; Fund for Investments in Basic Research) project "A multidimensional approach to technology transfer" and *Programmi di ricerca di interesse nazionale* (PRIN; Research Programs of National Interest) project "Italian Design System," both of the Italian Ministry for Education, Universities, and Research; and the European Union project "EVAN-European Value Networks."

Many colleagues and students provided us with invaluable help. Jim Utterback would like to thank Peter Grant and Eduardo Alvarez, students in the MIT Management of Technology Program, for the work represented in their thesis research for the project. At the Judge Business School, University of Cambridge, Dean Dame Sandra Dawson and Professor Nick Oliver provided indispensable hospitality and resources during Jim's recent sabbatical. The work benefited greatly from Jim's appointment as a visiting fellow by Professor Ekhard Salje and the Fellowship of Clare Hall, University of Cambridge, and the encouragement given by Professor Elizabeth Garnsey, his faculty sponsor at Clare Hall. Many ideas included in the book had their first glimmering in conversations with the late Chris Lorenz of the *Financial Times*, Al Lehnerd of the University of Pennsylvania, and Marc Meyer of Northeastern University. Other ideas were suggested in lectures given at MIT by Professor Russell Ackoff of the Wharton School, Tim Brown of IDEO, James Dyson, and Dean Kamen, inventor of the iBOT™. Ms. Alex Balkwill of the Centre for Competitiveness and Innovation at the Judge Business School, University of Cambridge, and Ms. Carolyn Mulaney at the MIT Sloan School of Management provided important help preparing the text, exhibits, bibliography, and notes.

Bengt-Arne Vedin notes that Professor Hans Rausing, KBE, has been a probing discussion partner throughout the project, and that Marcus Seppälä deserves kudos for the sketching series in Appendix B.

Susan Sanderson would like to thank Mastafa Uzumeri for his contribution to the development of the concept and early work on design classics. Bruce Tether would like to thank the directors of CRIC for supporting his research collaboration. Eduardo Alvarez would like to thank Dave Privitera and Douglas Dayton, heads of the IDEO office in Boston. Roberto Verganti led the entire group of authors to meet Ezio Manzini, Francesco Zurlo, Giuliano Simonelli from the School of Design of Politecnico di Milano, Ernesto Gismondi, Carlotta De Bevilacqua of Artemide in Milan, and independent design consultant Michele De Lucchi in 2002. These interviews were of great value, as was the participation of two students, Alessio Marchesi and Rossella Vacchelli, in different stages of the project.

The students in the Department of Innovation, Design & Product Development, Mälardalen University, created a lot of ideas and models for the multi-sport wheelchair project featured in Chapter 7. As inspiration and for a deeper understanding of designing wheelchairs, Sten Ekman and Susan Sanderson had a great deal of support from Professor Rory A. Cooper at the University of Pittsburgh and from lead users and product firm managers Bob Hall, Jalle Jungnell, Bo Lindkvist, and Tommy Olsson. We are grateful too to J. Douglas Field, Vice President for Product Development at Segway, who provided insight into the development of the iBOT.

Professor Koenraad Debackere of the University of Leuven provided warm hospitality for our meeting in conjunction with the International Product Development conference there in 2001. Our university departments and our partners Peggy, Gull-May, More, Annalill, Silvia, Arthur, and Francesca also provided great encouragement for our work and hospitality for our meetings. We thank all of our partners, colleagues and friends for their help.

The authors are most grateful to have had the skills of our outstanding editor, Scott Cooper, to help us in finishing our project successfully. A project involving so many authors with so many perspectives, as well as differing cultural and language traditions, presents special challenges. In addition to resolving many of the technical issues related to publishing a book, Scott has worked patiently with each of us to be sure that our work speaks with a unified voice and style. He has much improved the book by helping to draw themes consistently through the various chapters in a logical and cumulative manner. And he has helped the book to be clearer by debating the meanings and nuances of the work while being militant against jargon.

Finally, we are grateful to the people of the design firms and other organizations interviewed. We value the time and effort they invested on our behalf. Representatives of IDEO were interviewed in Boston, San Francisco, and London and of Design Continuum in Boston and Milan. Other American design firms interviewed included Altitude, Bleck Design Group, Herbst Lazar Bell, Manta Product Design, The Massachusetts Institute of Technology Media Laboratory and its AgeLab, Synectics, 9th Wave, Product Genesis, Product Insight, and Walt Disney. Italian companies interviewed included Artemide, Flos, Alessi, Kartell, B&B Italia, 3P3più, Snaidero, Mantero, Ferrero, Bang & Olufsen, LEGO®, Michele De Lucchi Design, Makio Hasuike, and Future Concept Lab. Swedish design firms interviewed were A&E Design, Caran, Ergonomidesign, Formbolaget,

Formtech, Go Solid, Hampf Design, Myra, No Picnic, Nya Perspektiv, Peekaboo Design, Propeller, Reload, Semcon, Stilpolisen, Struktur Industridesign, Ytterborn & Fuentes, White Design, Zenit Design, and Ångpanneföreningen. Representatives of the internal design facilities of Electrolux and Softronic were interviewed. Several clients of industrial design firms were also interviewed, including ABB Robotics, Artemide, ETAC, INSU Innovation Support, Tedak, the Swedish Telecommunications Museum/Telia Research AB, and Senseboard.

# ABOUT THE AUTHORS

**James M Utterback** is David J McGrath jr (1959) Professor of Management and Innovation in the Sloan School of Management and Professor of Engineering Systems in the School of Engineering at the Massachusetts Institute of Technology. He is a Fellow of the Royal Swedish Academy of Engineering Sciences and a Member of the Board of Governors of Argonne National Laboratory.

**Bengt-Arne Vedin** is Professor of Innovation Management at Mälardalen University in Eskilstuna, Sweden. He is a Fellow of the Royal Swedish Academy of Engineering Sciences, the Swedish Society for International Affairs, the Swedish Academy of Verbovisual Communication, and the World Academy of Art & Science.

**Eduardo Alvarez** is a graduate of MIT, where he did his thesis on *Managing Creativity for Effective Innovation*. He is a designer and entrepreneur and is President of VIGIX, Inc, which he founded.

**Sten Ekman**, Doctor of Industrial Ergonomics, is at the Department of Innovation, Design and Product Development at Mälardalen University in

Eskilstuna, Sweden. He has been honored as "The Entrepreneur of the Year in Academic Leadership in Sweden 2001" and also for the Mälardalen Program on Innovation Management as "The Entrepreneurial Program of the Year in Sweden 2000." He is the head of an international four-year project "University Business Development Centres at Ukrainian Universities" from 2005.

**Susan Walsh Sanderson** is Associate Professor at the Lally School of Management at Rensselaer Polytechnic Institute in Troy, New York. She is recipient of the Boeing Outstanding Educator Award and the Hesburg Award for Educational Innovation.

**Bruce Tether** is Professor of Innovation Management and Strategy at the Centre for Research on Innovation and Competition, Manchester Business School and a Ghoshal Fellow of the United Kingdom's Advanced Institute of Management Research.

**Roberto Verganti** is Professor of Management of Innovation at the School of Management and at the Faculty of Design of Politecnico di Milano, and Director of MaDe In Lab, the laboratory for Marketing, Design and Innovation of MIP-School of Management of Politecnico di Milano. He is a Member of the Scientific Committee of the European Institute for Advanced Studies in Management, and Member of the Advisory Council of the Design Management Institute, Boston. A project *Sistema Design Italia* in which he participated as a Member of the Scientific Organizing Committee was awarded the most prestigious design award in Italy, the *"Compasso d'Oro"* in 2001.

# Chapter 1

## *WHAT MAKES PRODUCTS GREAT?*

A design-inspired product *delights* the customer. The product emphasizes sophisticated simplicity and economy of means and low impact. If a product's use is apparent, simple, and clear, it will stand out from all those that compete for our attention. Great products are those that have grown in meaning and value over their — and generations of users' — lifetimes. They capture our hearts and make our lives easier, better, or more interesting. Elegant products live on long after trivial variations have been relegated to the trash heap.

Design-inspired innovation requires creativity of a higher order, whether the products are professional tools, machinery for production, consumer goods, or services. It is, in essence, a synthesis of technology and users' experiences — boundaries that we observe blurring. Increasingly, products succeed because they have associated software and services that enhance their value. In the end, what the user remembers is a delightful experience with the entire package, and not whether that experience was provided or enabled by any particular aspect of the design.

Most innovation improves products along accepted trajectories of higher performance and lower cost. By contrast, strikingly innovative products broaden and change the boundaries of performance, usefulness, and meaning. Few designs result in products that create such dramatic market success that they drive a company's overall competitive strategy. People today hunger for products that offer more than sufficient function, high quality, and low cost. Even superb functionality no longer assures success for a new product. To achieve inspired designs and innovations, the aspiration must be for excellence and elegance. Excellence is achieved when a product is eminently good. Elegance — the tasteful richness of a product's design — is achieved when a product is neat and simple.

Customers do not necessarily want a wide variety, but they do want what is exactly the right choice for them. There is a growing richness of variety in the component supply environment, which enables greater creativity, combination, and experiment at the system level, but at the same time widens competition, doubly so when new materials and software capabilities are considered. Modularity means that we have the growing ability to design and produce products for small markets or even for a single customer. An example, a new concept for a riding saddle, is explained in detail below.

Design-inspired innovations seem to be aimed primarily at elite consumers in highly developed economies, but we believe that there is no reason to maintain such an excessively narrow focus. Design-inspired innovation creates products that have meaning. Many people strive toward a world of greater beauty, humanity, and ethics, as well as one that provides basic necessities — and we sense a rapidly growing wave of interest in creating more meaningful products that also reduce waste and reside easily in our natural and cultural environments. In the developing world, greater numbers of people aspire to have the goods and services enjoyed in developed economies, while even greater numbers aspire simply to have basic products and services. More products seem to emphasize sophisticated simplicity rather than just a welter of features, and more products seem to emphasize economy of means and low impact rather than simply economy alone.

For example, Tim Brown, head of IDEO, noted his company's success in developing a disposable injection pen for providing insulin inexpensively to help diabetics. Examples in later chapters include a simple and effective emergency shelter and less wasteful designs for food packaging. Groups such as Britain's Sorrell Foundation and MIT's AgeLab are searching for approaches to provide better experiences and products for both younger and older clients.

Our thesis is that design-inspired products, those with both excellence and elegance, will be both more profitable and enduring. Of course, there are worries. Christopher Lorenz, in his seminal 1986 work on corporate use of design, warned:

> "[T]he trouble is that right does not always triumph, and principles are not always borne out in practice. Existing deterrents against the fully-fledged use of industrial design in many companies could take on new significance if globalization is managed badly. Design would then be pushed back to the dark ages of skin-deep styling, and the companies would be deprived of that 'meaningful distinction' which, as

Theodore Levitt rightly argues, is so crucial to the creation of competitive advantage in an era of crowded markets and global competition."[1]

Ironically, the best products may be the ones that disappear almost entirely: the human light, the music library, the wheelchair, a waste handling system. All of these, and other examples, are presented in detail in subsequent chapters, where we put what makes them "best" in the context of excellence and elegance.

Design, especially its integration with other functions of a firm and its strategy, has received less emphasis in previous research than is merited by its importance for success in a competitive environment. For example, as Procter & Gamble CEO A.G. Lafley, says:

> "I've been in this business for almost thirty years, and it's always been functionally organized. So where does design go? We want to design the purchasing experience — what we call the 'first moment of truth'; we want to design every component of the product; and we want to design the communication experience and the user experience."[2]

Where, indeed, does design go? We will argue that it must constitute the beginning of the innovation process and consider the totality of a product's use and life rather than the design process being one in which the product is just conceived as an artifact or an implement.

**What is design-inspired innovation?**

**How does it lead to competitive advantage?**

A growing number of companies recognize the importance of design-inspired innovation, especially those that aim to strengthen and maintain high product value. These companies are willing to take the large risks associated with this quite complex and uncertain approach. To answer the questions above requires taking the widely acknowledged definition of design as the integrated innovation of function and form and adapting it further to the framework illustrated in Exhibit 1.1.

The Exhibit shows graphically that three types of knowledge are essential to the innovation process — knowledge about user needs, technological opportunities, and product languages. The last component concerns the signs that can be used to deliver a message to the

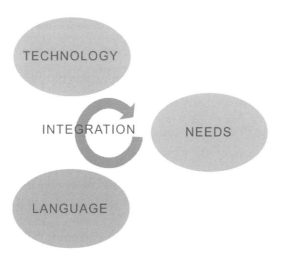

**Exhibit 1.1.** Design as the integration of technology, needs, and language. Adapted from Verganti, 2003.

user and the cultural context in which the user will give meaning to those signs. The classic dialectic of function versus form leads designers to relegate the latter to the aesthetic appearance of products. Indeed, the debate often focuses simplistically on the contrast between functionalism and styling — particularly in industries such as furniture and lighting, where aesthetic content is considered to be the key driver of competition. Exhibit 1.1 expands and elaborates the concept that great design captures the meaning of products, as well as function and customer needs.

In design-inspired innovation, the balance among technology, market and meaning is unique. None can be neglected. Rather, balance results from a vision about a *possible* future. In Chapter 4, we refer to this as an "ideal design."

What really matters to the user, in addition to functionality, is a product's emotional and symbolic value — its meaning. If functionality aims at satisfying the operative needs of the customer, the product's meaning tickles one's emotional and socio-cultural needs. As Virginia Postrel argues:

> "… ultimately, the only way to mitigate aesthetic conflicts is to establish design boundaries that recognize the wide variety of people and the impossibility of deducing from aesthetic principles what individuals will, or should, value. We have to return to Adam Smith: to accept the importance of specialization and to understand that a large market of many people need

not be a mass market of homogeneous goods. Good design boundaries ... will embrace pluralism."[3]

Lorenz argues that this may seem like trying to have it both ways, but that a critical factor in design is to manage and balance just such ambiguity.

How can a firm achieve a design-inspired innovation? How can it define new meanings that are successful in the marketplace? To answer these questions, let us first look generally at innovation as the result of a process of generating and integrating knowledge.

Product and service design should not be an isolated function within a company. Rather, it should involve every single aspect of the company working together on the entire customer experience. That experience begins the moment the customer first comes into contact with the product, perhaps in a showroom or an advertisement, and continues through every aspect of the interaction across the life of the product or the length of the service. This illustrates that the product itself is only a *part* of the experience — in some cases, a small part. It is critical, then, that product design teams include members with diverse knowledge of finance, marketing, service, logistics, and other functions.

A *Business Week* article argued: "[A]s the economy shifts from the economies of scale to the economics of choice and as mass markets fragment and brand loyalty disappears, it is more important than ever for corporations to improve the 'consumer experience.' "[4] This shift can be seen at design firms such as IDEO, where, as CEO Tim Brown said in a presentation at MIT: "[T]he firm has moved strategically from designing products, to designing services, to currently designing entire customer experiences with products and services."

Procter & Gamble is now IDEO's largest single customer. IDEO has moved beyond products, services, and customer experiences to an attempt to help Procter & Gamble itself design a culture to foster greater innovation. As head A.G. Lafley, who is attempting to put design "into the DNA" of Procter & Gamble, says:

> "I think it is value that rules the world. There is … evidence across many categories that consumers will pay more for a better design, better performance, better quality, better value, and better experiences. Our biggest discussion item with … retailers is getting them to understand that price is part of it, but in many cases not the deciding factor."[5]

Product designers, then, must become designers of the customer experience. The Apple iPod, discussed in Chapter 2, offers a prime example. The device itself is nicely designed, but its most important competitive advantage is its seamless integration with more important aspects of the customer experience, such as the iTunes website where content is easily made available to the user. Significantly, the newest service offered as part of the content provided on an iPod, the so-called "Podcast," was neither designed nor created by Apple. Rather, it is a creation of a user community encouraged and enabled by Apple's use of standard connections in its product and open standards for its content provision. Podcasts now provide not only time-shifted news and broadcast content of all sorts, but myriad other possibilities from museum audio tours to updates about family events.

More successful designs often involve an extended ensemble of services and accessories that enhance and reinforce the users' experiences. These may arise through open standards or user communities that encourage users and partners to develop them. Likewise, design firms that work on products that a customer can use easily and in which function is amplified through attendant accessories, systems, and services will be more successful than others.

**What strategies encourage design-inspired innovation?**

Success in design-inspired innovation requires a broad search for information and robust experimentation, with lots of feedback from customers on both steps. Designers who create modular designs allow greater variety and experimentation at lower cost per experiment, thus creating a greater chance of learning quickly from failure, and in turn heightening the chances of success. Likewise, design firms that introduce a greater number of prototypes may grow more rapidly than those that maintain a tight focus. Modular design is a pre-condition for so-called mass customization. With readily connected modules, customers can more easily select the modules that provide an ensemble of preferred features. According to Joe Pine, the most ingenious companies provide design software and services (or "design tools") that readily allow customers to visualize the result of a selected combination.[6] This idea is discussed in more detail in Chapter 4.

## Seeking and Experimenting

Clearly, design-inspired innovation might involve much more seeking and experimenting than planning. Great designs might be those that provide for more variations to meet particular customer needs or specifications, or for more variations to be tried quickly in the marketplace to zero in on the version most highly suited to customer needs and preferences. "The work of Scherer (1999) shows that returns from innovation are highly skewed. Only a few innovations in a portfolio produce significantly above-average returns. Similarly, only a small number of academic publications get very highly cited, a small number of patents produce most income, and a small number of products yield the majority of sales. Although the performance of incremental innovations tends to be less skewed than radical innovations, the implications of these skewed returns are clear: as Scherer argues, the chances of success in innovation are such that an appropriate metaphor is that of a lottery. Spending more on innovation, or buying more tickets, provides more chances of success but large expenditure does not ensure that you win."[7]

We believe greater value is being created more consistently by innovation at the systems level, rather than at the components level. The most powerful designs appear to be those that are architectural and modular — they are defined by creating new *ensembles* of components and connections among them, rather than simply adding new components. Architectural designs in particular often broaden the application of a product or open up entirely new uses for it, thus rapidly expanding the market.

Functional innovation is only rarely based on radically new technology. More frequently, it is a cumulative, incremental improvement of existing components and extension of established product architectures. Given that, there appears to be much potential value in reconsidering products "inside the envelope" with a fresh eye and approach. A wonderful example is a new saddle designed for competitive riders, or, more accurately, a saddle *system* for both horse and rider that may serve to illustrate many of the points made thus far.

### Linear's Saddle, Designed for Both Rider and Horse

Most saddles today are modeled on a form established at least 500 years ago, and some 60 percent of riding horses suffer from back problems because saddles aren't designed to distribute human weight. The lives of these horses are shorter than necessary. The saddle design we encountered through our interviews in Sweden addresses these problems through a totally new saddle concept.

Linear — working with Stockholm-based design firm Propeller — has created a totally new saddle concept. Designed for an anatomically healthy horse's spine and movements, the Horseback-Modular Saddle System is ergonomically suited for both the horse and rider. The innovative design breaks new ground in a conservative product category by using new materials and industrial production.

The starting point is to consider horse and rider as one *system*. The saddle should be adaptable to individual differences among horse and load. The rider's weight should be distributed as evenly as possible over as large an area as possible, so as not to restrict the horse's blood circulation.

Linear's saddle is *modular*, with the lower part for the horse's back and the upper module for the rider and the actual riding discipline (see Exhibit 1.2). This allows the rider to switch easily between different disciplines, and eliminates the costly need for multiple saddles. The lower saddle is made not of the traditional leather but a lightweight carbon fiber, which makes for an extraordinarily light 2-pound product and distributes pressure evenly over the horse's back — at a much lower production cost. At the same time, the saddle allows for good ventilation of the horse's back. The main advantage: a happier, healthier horse.

The saddle design shows clearly the combination of modularity, customization, systems thinking, and inspiration within a basic system that provides saddles beautifully tailored to both horse and rider. The customer is delighted.

We cannot overstress our view that a company's entire strategy should be focused on this single objective: *delighting the customer*. In today's globally competitive world, it should be expected that some other company will — with relative ease — come along and fill a space void of delight, pushing other companies out of business. Delight

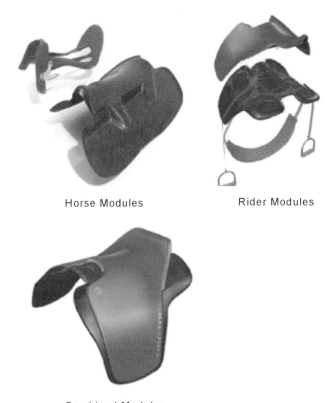

Horse Modules                    Rider Modules

Combined Modules

**Exhibit 1.2.** Propeller design's saddle for rider and horse.

transcends reliability and simplicity to achieve something greater than the sum of the parts.

**Why is simplicity key to achieving customer delight?**

Simplicity and elegance are ignored at a company's peril. Our lives are amazingly complex, and complexity is stressful. Modern life is an equation with multiple variables: work, family, relationships, finances, hobbies, education, emergencies, health, maintenance, compliance, expectations, taxes, and so on. As difficult as it is to keep current with all these variables, it is even more difficult to *control* them in the way we want. Simplicity eases some of the burden and creates space for enjoyment. A product that is simple to use allows us to enjoy what it does.

Why, then, are most products and services *not* simple? Why does a new digital camera come with a 200-page user manual? Complexity is a grand temptation for designers because, more often than not, it is a means by which to compensate for or mask poor design. An architect might compensate for a poor or uninspired house design with moldings, textures, and colors. "It makes sense intuitively," write Rust, Thompson, and Hamilton, "that an overload of features detracts from a product's usability. It's also been proven over and over again in research."[8] Similarly, a product designer tends to add features and ornaments to hide fundamental deficiencies in his design. What else explains, for example, the ubiquitous echo feature on surround-sound home audio amplifiers that makes a movie viewed at home sound the same as watching it in a stadium?

Perhaps "... engineers can't resist the temptation to equip existing electronic components with more functions. Of course, they are not looking at the whole equation, which includes the intangible costs of reduced usability."[9] In short, designers often confuse or confound desirable attributes such as beauty, elegance, and quality with extra features and ornamentation. "The experience of using a product changes the equation underlying consumers' preferences ... Put simply, what looks attractive in prospect does not necessarily look good in practice. Consumers often become frustrated and dissatisfied with the very cornucopia of features they originally desired and chose."[10]

## Simplicity: The Case of Two Search Engines

A comparison of two search engines on the World Wide Web — Yahoo® and Google® — affords an illustration of the power and desirability of *simplicity*. Yahoo offers a vast categorization system, but at an early point in the process it is quite easy to forget what the original search was for. Yahoo forces the user to browse through dozens of links, advertisements, and unneeded information. Google, however, provides a straightforward, focused, and *simple* user experience.

Google achieved this simplicity in part with the approach the company took to developing its search engine product. "When we started," explains Sergey Brin, Google co-founder, "we didn't have a webmaster. The result was a nice, simple interface. And we stayed true to that because we realized it helps people get their searches done faster. They don't want to hang out on a home page when they want to get information quickly." Keeping the development team small helped avoid over-engineering Google's web interface.

It is Google's simplicity and reliability that has allowed the company to achieve an amazingly large share of the US web search industry. According to the July 2005 Nielsen NetRatings, 54 percent of web searches were performed at Google.[11] Yahoo came in a distant second, with only 23 percent — despite Yahoo's being a larger company with more resources. A 2003 survey offers further proof that users respond to simplicity. "Google, the powerful search tool that presents Internet surfers with a minimum of visual clutter, came top in a global poll of 1,315 respondents to a survey by Interbrand, a leading British branding agency."[12]

Google's simplicity is not only about its user interface, but also has to do with the company's technology and even its very business model. Everything has been designed with one thing in mind: the customer is looking for *precise* information and wants it *fast*.

Still, Google confronts the dilemma of trying to grow while preserving simplicity. "That famously Spartan user interface is about to face a major test as the outfit seeks to drum up attention for its many new offerings," reports *Business Week*. "Change has been one of the only constants at Google. In five years, its payroll has rocketed from about 100 to over 4,200 staffers. Sales have jumped from $19 million to more than $3 billion. And its product offerings have mushroomed from simple Internet search to include dozens more, from e-mail to maps to instant messaging. Despite this roiling change, Google's famously minimalist home page looks almost as it did when the upstart search company owned just 1 percent of the market."[13]

Even those companies that achieve the kind of simplicity that generates customer delight can find it difficult to remain faithful to the simplicity principle. Time and again, companies that owe their initial success to the simplicity of products they design "kill the golden goose" as they exhibit the seemingly natural tendency to make the next generations increasingly complex.

"New England villages are admirable because they are limited. They were built in tight confines, against the surrounding wilderness. They were built of the simplest materials: wood, nails, plaster, bricks, stone, mortar and glass ... The graceful place is born of limits: in material, knowledge and time." — Howard Mansfield[14]

Examples abound: consider Quickbooks accounting software, Palm Pilot personal digital assistants, and the Windows operating system. These products were category killers because they were simple and easy to use, but the companies, feeling the pressure to grow, pushed their designers to create more complex new versions — in other words, to add "bells and whistles." Systems engineers cynically call this phenomenon the "second system syndrome," meaning that once something is working in a well thought out first version, everyone's favorite idea or feature is thrown into a cumbersome second version.

Designers who want to stay true to the simplicity principle must acknowledge the need for constant discipline to prevent the urge for more short term sales that lead to disappointment and declining sales later. Reed and his colleagues note that BMW's overly complex dashboard, with a huge number of options, has led to a 10 percent sales decline in 2005.[15] Simplicity is even more compelling because most developed countr ies confront aging populations (which, we posit, appreciate, and indeed require simplicity), as we detail in Chapter 4.

## How is the innovation process changing?

All of this discussion points to changes in the innovation process among companies and industries — for better or worse. We perceive a growing trend to view design in the same light as contract manufacturing has been viewed for more than a century. The increasing pressure on corporations for financial performance encourages companies to contract out all activities that are seen to provide no competitive advantage. Each of the design firms we interviewed concurred that they were also seeing more design contracting. One firm offered that "it's a huge pond" regarding growth in the product development industry.[16] There is other evidence of firms seeking outside assistance, through design contracting, to acquire capabilities they do not themselves possess. The use of outside design services is growing in the United States, Japan, and other countries.[17] Tim Brown of IDEO noted in an early 2006 presentation at MIT that there is a movement from small partnerships centered around one individual toward more organized and integrated firms and collaborations.

In his "Open Innovation" study, Henry Chesbrough suggests that the innovation process has shifted from a closed process within corporations toward an open process drawing on many sources of knowledge. He notes that "companies can find vital knowledge in customers, suppliers, universities, national labs, consortia, consultants, and even start-up firms."[18] Applying this connect and develop concept, Larry Huston and Nabil Sakkab of Procter & Gamble demonstrate how the company has in just five years gone from 15 percent of external product origination to 35 percent, toward a goal of 50 percent. R&D productivity has jumped by 60 percent, and the innovation success rate more than doubled.[19]

The clients of product development firms know that their competitors are getting technology from many different sources, including design firms. Therefore, some firms have linked a competitive benefit to contracting for design. The bilateral transfer of knowledge during design collaboration for competitive advantage is a phenomenon that is both obvious and subtle. Of course, both the client and the product design firm can learn from one another during the design of a product, but the subtlety lies in recognizing this fact so that it can be exploited through knowledge management practices. What we observe, as noted at the beginning of this chapter, is a more network-centered innovation process, involving a greater number of actors, including users, design firms, and consultants. Increased networking is aided both by the increasing popularity of open standards and open source forms of development, and by the greater prevalence of sophisticated design tools which augment the capabilities of smaller groups and organizations.

Firms tend to search locally, and innovation efforts tend to be amplified by the presence of diverse local partners and connections. Sources of innovation are not uniformly distributed, but rather are concentrated in a few regions of sophisticated demand and expertise. In some cases, such "clusters" are becoming distributed, or "virtual," but are still characterized by rich connectedness among actors and agents. A gathered cluster of suppliers and customers makes design firms more viable, and vice versa. While the cluster environment is the same for all firms, each individual firm will differ in terms of number and strength of linkages to other players. More successful firms will include both customers and suppliers within their design activities, as illustrated in Exhibit 1.3. At the same time, they will be different enough from their customers in culture and action to bring them fresh perspective and direction in product development.

In summary, the innovation process has become more networked and involves a greater number of actors — users, design firms, and suppliers. Open standards and the increasing use of open source innovation seem to be spreading roles across — indeed, breaking down — boundaries. Many design firms now also provide turnkey services for new products and even for entire product lines. That is, in addition to product design, they are more actively providing manufacturers with material and component choices as well as sources of supply and marketing concepts.

**What is to follow?**

All of these observations are made more explicit in our discussion throughout the book. Chapter 2, "Creating Design Classics," presents the common features of elegant "classic" models. One such feature is often the creation of formal and informal communities of users and accessory

A Traditional Firm                    A Contemporary Firm in a Dynamic Network

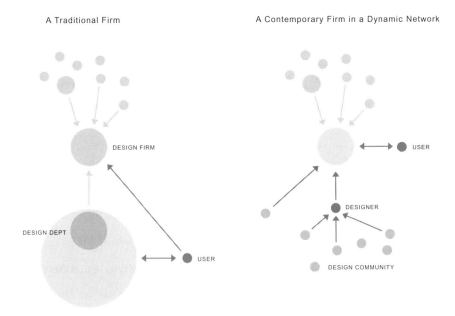

**Exhibit 1.3.** Movement toward networks and brokering of design services.

providers. In the chapter, we also analyze and illustrate the economic value of outstanding design, noting that a mere 5 percent of models of several products garner the lion's share of profits. These classic models last nearly twice as long in the market as other examples.

In Chapter 3, "Integrating Function and Design," we contend that research on the economics of innovation and technological change is too concentrated on research-intensive activities. Our focus here is on design activities, and within that more particularly on product design activities, often overlooked when dealing with what is termed as "research and development." The chapter is based in large part on a survey of firms in the United Kingdom, where a sizable effort is vested in what is described as "silent design." It is interesting to note the positive correlation between economic performance and design interpreted more broadly.

The anecdotal evidence to suggest that independent design firms are playing an increasingly important role is presented in Chapter 4, "Managing the Design Process." These firms are supplying innovation to corporate America, as we discuss. Given that it is normal for the leader at one stage of technology to lose out to a newcomer at the next stage, how might design affect this pattern of passing the baton? What are the lessons from successes in designing entire systems, thinking in architectures and modules rather than single products? We provide an in-depth description of how an innovation project has been carried out in conjunction with a leading industrial design consultancy.

Chapter 4 advocates taking a step back to get a larger view, and in Chapter 5, "The Work of Designers," we draw lessons from Swedish design consultancies — some of which suggest "starting from dreams" and "thinking the impossible" as part of the design process. Almost all Swedish design firms perform innovation services integrated into their design work for their customers. These services form part of a larger menu of offerings: the country or the firms do not offer a scale sufficient for narrow specialization.

Thus, our interviews in Sweden give us a good opportunity to view the process in the larger context. Broader context also is often their recipe for servicing their clients: taking a life cycle approach; designing a corporate image; a corporate strategy; a value chain. Bringing in knowledge from starkly different industries is an important quality, as is staying close to scientific and technology breakthroughs.

Chapter 6 details "The Design Discourse," focusing on Italy. Successful Italian manufacturers in design-intensive industries owe much of their success to unique capabilities in mastering design-driven innovation in messages transcending form and function. Italian firms appear to have developed capabilities to understand, anticipate, and influence the emergence of new product meanings. The discourse referred to takes place in a greater Milan design system, transcending what is normally seen as a resource dependent cluster. Designers in Milan and Lombardy interpret and are affected by cultural signals and stimuli shared with, among others, publishers and advertising agencies. The design systems view also informs the interaction between design firms in Massachusetts and its industrial substrate (Chapter 4) as it does for the Swedish transportation technology and industrial engineering systems respectively (Chapter 5).

The lessons of the Italian experience inform, to a large extent, our overall conception of design-inspired innovation and the guidelines we develop in our final chapter.

In Chapter 7, we take off from the concept of "messages" discussed in Chapter 6 and provide an extended example of design influencing innovation in a particular product arena. This chapter, "Broadening Human Possibilities Through Design," focuses on innovative sports wheelchairs. For a disabled person, a wheelchair is inarguably an implement with *meaning*. The chapter illustrates the extent to which functions, components, and design features, first tried and tested in a demanding sports environment, spill over into "ordinary" active wheelchairs, promising great future demand from the growing elderly population in the world. It further highlights that the design of a product is a statement about the product's owner: why should someone disabled be shut out of sports? Intelligently, elegantly designed technology comes to the rescue.

Chapter 8, "Design — Vision and Visualizing," explores alternative design processes being used by design firms for the development of products in order to elucidate the changing nature of practices in the pursuit of outstanding products. As we have discovered, the traditional adage that form follows function no longer works. However, visualization or form is certainly at the core of design and designing. Sketches allow for efficient communication and for provoking bold ideas. Visualization turns out to complement more established analytical tools and, with the advent of computers as well as new insights into how our minds work, holds out promises for entirely new opportunities to arrive at elegant products and services.

Our aim is to promote the wider diffusion of tools and practices, including effective alliances between manufacturing firms and design firms to create more widespread, successful product designs. Thus, we end the book with what we believe are valuable guidelines to assess and predict the effectiveness of product development and design processes.

**Endnotes**

---

[1]C. Lorenz, 1986 (Revised 1990), p. 141; citing T. Levitt, 1986, p. 128.

[2]Quoted in J. Reingold, 2005, p. 56.

[3]V. Postrel, 2005, p. 146.

[4]B. Nussbaum, 2004.

[5]Reingold, 2005.

[6]Pine II, B.J., 1993.

[7]M. Dodgson, D. Gann, and A. Salter, 2005, p. 16.

[8]R.T. Rust, D.V. Thompson, and R.W. Hamilton, 2006, p. 100.

[9]Rust, Thompson, and Hamilton, 2006, p. 100.

[10]Rust, Thompson, and Hamilton, 2006, p. 104.

[11]On the basis of search provider.

[12]T. Datson, 2003.

[13]BusinessWeek Online, 2005.

[14]H. Mansfield, 2000.

[15]R.T. Rust et al., 2006.

[16]E. Gilchrest, 2000.

[17]P.L. Grant, 2000.

[18]H. Chesbrough, 2003, p. 40.

[19]L. Huston and N. Sakkab, 2006, pp. 58–66.

# Chapter 2

## *CREATING DESIGN CLASSICS**

With so little certainty about the prospects for individual designs, and with markets fragmenting into smaller segments, manufacturers must generate more and more models. It stands to reason, therefore, that they look aggressively for ways to identify and develop winning designs *intentionally*. Are there identifiable factors that *cause* products to be successful or unsuccessful?

Scholars have been investigating the reasons for new product success or failure for at least four decades. Much of the research has focused on *causal* factors of success, including customer satisfaction, the novelty of the product, and the efficiency of the development process, as well as failure factors, including misreading of markets, the actions of competitors, and technical problems.[1] The evidence suggests strongly that no *single* factor determines the outcomes of competitive innovation. To be successful, companies must consider a host of factors and select the objectives and approaches that are likely to be most effective for their specific product.

For example, it is easy to generalize that products should evoke a perception of value in potential customers. It is difficult, however, to

*This chapter is a substantially revised and amplified version of S. Sanderson and V. Uzumeri, 1997, Chapter 9.

make generalizations about the design features that are likely to create that perception. A customer's definition of value is bound tightly to the specifics of the individual design and the proposed application.

### Finding Patterns: The Research

Several detailed industry case studies helped pave the way for uncovering the patterns we discuss. Abernathy and Utterback's research on early automobile industry innovation introduced the concept of *dominant design* as competition between early concepts (e.g., steam vs. electric vs. diesel vs. gasoline engines).[2] Maidique and Zirger's study showed that companies might have to fail at least once to learn enough about the design and market interaction to create a successful design.[3] Von Hippel's search for the sources of innovation identified the important role *users of technology* often play.[4] Henderson and Clark's study of successive generations of semiconductor equipment manufacturers illustrated how design inertia could prevent leading companies from switching to newer and better technologies.[5] Christensen suggests that established firms often fall into the trap of continuing to pursue product performance along traditional dimensions when customers might be better served by less refined or "disruptive" technology with broader functionality.[6] Von Hippel contends that where innovation takes place is shifting toward users over time — a starting point for our work. We would expand the notion of "users" to include design firms and the creative community, broadly conceived.[7]

Prescriptions concerning success and failure, while quite valuable to the practicing innovation manager, add little to our understanding about broader *patterns* of successful innovation.

More and more researchers have conducted detailed industry case studies to uncover relevant patterns. From these studies, a picture has begun to emerge of a competitive environment where new products are developed and prosper in a complex game governed by definable rules.

Some products are inherently short-lived, offering no hope of long-term sales, whereas others hold the promise of enduring sales. Companies that establish a *pattern* of model development that can both exploit and withstand market uncertainty seem to do best with their product design. We see such a pattern with the Sony Walkman, portable computers, and computer workstations. Each product family contained many models — some that were replaced rapidly and others that survived for a considerable period.

Too little change opens the door to competitors who take advantage of advances in materials and dropping prices. Too much change makes customers confused by a vast number of products with little to differentiate one from another. Firms must find the balance, with a product range that takes advantage of advances in technology without confusing customers with poorly designed and executed models. A few firms have excelled in creating outstanding and memorable models — iconic products that have raised the company value. Apple's iPod and Artemide's Tizio lamp come to mind as products that have achieved iconic status and helped their respective firms achieve great financial success.

## The design classic

Certain product models — what Sanderson and Uzumeri first called "business classics"[8] and we are now referring to as design classics — may be long-lived and a substantial part of a firm's overall, long-term success. Design classics play an important role in the development of the firm's product family and may even influence the design direction of the category as a whole.

It is important to differentiate between a design classic and a classic design. For instance, the Mazda Miata discussed later in this chapter is a design classic, whereas the 1955 Studebaker is a classic design of a car. To be sure, the Studebaker remains sleek, elegant, and beautiful. Designers and design critics can wax lyrical over it for hours, and do so in books. But it did not make Studebaker a best-selling car. A *design classic* is long-lived.

Some products are design classics because of their extraordinary historical *impact* on industries, markets, and even economies. Examples include the IBM 360 series mainframe computer, Xerox dry copier, and Intel's microprocessor. Some of these product families were quite revolutionary when introduced. Business interest in radical innovation is understandable. A radical design that achieves a durable market presence saps competitors' market share and revenues. The innovator sees revenues rise and costs fall and enjoys a favorable cash flow (and the warm glow of success bathes many of the innovator's other products and businesses). Products representing radical designs spawn new product families and trigger new rounds of competition.

**What is Product Longevity?**

The terminology associated with the notion of product longevity complicates discussion of long-lived design. In a reference to a "lengthy" product lifecycle, what is being measured? "Product" could be construed to be a technology, brand, type of design, or even a specific model, which complicates matters even more (e.g., a long-lived model typically has a much shorter life than the shortest-lived technology). In certain contexts, the term "longevity" embraces both *concepts* and *aspects of design* that are transferable from model to model and even across different products (e.g., any product that depicts Mickey Mouse). Even the appealingly simple term "classic" is too often confused with style and aesthetics. In this chapter, we aim to provide a more precise definition.

While the most revolutionary product designs get the bulk of the attention, the vast majority of new products are more ordinary. A few, though, rival or exceed the market impact of major technological breakthroughs. There are at least two major categories of incremental design longevity. Product *systems*, the first category, combine the state-of-the-art with predecessor technologies in significantly new arrangements. We can go all the way back to Ford's Model T for an example of what was, technologically, an incremental innovation.[9] It drew upon design components already used in other automobiles to create a vehicle that universally outperformed the donors. Other products characterized by technical designs more incremental than radical have enjoyed the equivalent of the Model T's historic market impact and longevity: for example, the original IBM PC and Volkswagen's Beetle, both of which were continuously updated and improved and which were offered to consumers at a very attractive price.

The second category of incremental design successes comprises the long-lived products that have come more broadly to be called "classics." These strictly incremental innovations lay no claim to technological novelty except perhaps when they were introduced, yet somehow bond so well with customers as to assure continued production even after they are no longer novel. Examples include the Kodak carousel slide projector, Harley-Davidson motorcycle, Rolodex rotary card file, and Levi jeans. We would argue that these products, in some way, meet our criteria for products that *delight* their users.

Some products retain their popularity for decades with little or no functional updating. The success of firms that developed these beloved products has been based largely on the ability to manage a few long-lived models that provide the bulk of their revenues. Moreover, they have been able to build important brands out of those designs. The intensely competitive toy industry, famous for very short product lifecycles, is the home of a few, including Crayola® crayons and LEGO® building blocks, which have remained favorites among generations of children.

Crayola and its original model, a box of eight crayons, made its first appearance more than 100 years ago. Two cousins produced a wax-based crayon, the most important aspect of which was its non-toxicity. The wife of one was an elementary school teacher and recognized the potential market, but no one could have anticipated the success of the crayon. Today, Crayola produces crayons packaged in boxes of eight to 120 individual crayons that are sold in more than 80 countries and in 12 languages. In its history, the company has sold hundreds of millions of crayons.

While there are many competing crayons on the market, Crayola has been incredibly successful in managing its core product family, and the firm is one of the world's best brand managers. The company has made a virtue out of continuity, and even retains the simple logo from when the product was introduced. Crayola is one of the most recognized brands worldwide. The Crayola name is recognized by 99 percent of Americans; incredibly, a Yale University study found that the Crayola crayon scent is the 18th most recognized scent to American adults.

Like Crayola, LEGO has done an outstanding job of managing its core product and brand. LEGO began in Denmark during the 1930s economic crisis. Since then, the original classic block design that appeals to pre-school children has remained the same, while it has been complemented with dozens of additional product lines popular with older girls and boys. In the more than 70 years since the blocks were introduced, over 190 billion pieces have been sold and LEGO has become Europe's largest toy manufacturer — despite some tough going in recent years.

Both Crayola and LEGO have been careful to protect the integrity of the classic products that form the basis for their brands and for their success. Novel when introduced, Crayola crayons and LEGO building blocks still speak to the needs of the market as well as they did at the time they were launched. The companies that created them have been careful not to make changes. Customers love that continuity, which gives them the opportunity to share with new generations their love for these classic products and the memories they evoke. Meanwhile, the companies balance this attention to maintaining the continuity of their core products with efforts to enhance the experience using those products with new technology. For example, LEGO is using new technology to enhance the experience for older children.

### LEGO Innovation with Design

Radically softening sales almost turned LEGO into a basket case. However, some drastic measures — some related specifically to product design — seem to be brightening the horizon.

LEGO has traditionally been open to new technology and various types of partnerships; the links to Seymour Papert at the MIT Media Lab, with his LEGO Logo, is a good example. Recently, the company developed customized CAD software that allows the user to design a structure virtually, using LEGO, and then order the precise set of parts to produce the construction. The LEGO website allows for uploading of designs so they may be shared with other LEGO builders; if a particular design turns out to be very popular, LEGO can decide to produce ready-made sets for their catalogue. "Today," says a LEGO spokesperson, "we employ 100 designers working on new LEGO structures. With this, we'll have 100,000."

It wasn't long after its introduction on the LEGO website that the software, called Digital Designer, was hacked by LEGO enthusiasts. Hackers made it possible for customers using the program to order less-costly tailor-made sets of LEGO parts. Unlike most corporations, LEGO welcomed the hacking. Now the company is contemplating the introduction of software specifically geared to allowing users to tinker with Digital Designer. LEGO is confident that its customers will come up with tricks and treats that the company itself would not have conceived.

Another means back to financial health also has to do with design: the complete redesign of the components for making LEGO robots — which cater mostly to adults, not children.

The best design practitioners try to learn from the past and are often inspired from previous classics. Hence, some classics are "retro." Mazda's MX-5 (also known as the Miata) is one product that has successfully recaptured the lost magic of the past. Initial work on the new sports car began in 1982 with a historical analysis of sports cars in America since 1945. As Yamaguchi and Thompson[10] explain, Mazda looked at American GIs' experiences with sports cars during World War II, as well as post-war imports of the MG, Triumph, and Jaguar — all front-engine, rear-drive convertibles with relatively long noses. "First impressions" from this period, the study concluded, are the most persistent images of sports cars in the minds of most Americans. The study also concluded that image is essential to a sports car's success and most successful sports cars have developed cult-like followings. Further, the findings suggested that a sports car needs to possess uniqueness, something that will capture the fancy of a segment of the population given to making impulse purchases. The car must be sexy (in the eyes of the typical auto buyer), fun-to-drive, exhibit good (if not spectacular) performance, and be offered at an affordable price.

When the Mazda MX-5 debuted at the Chicago Motor Show in February 1989, it was hailed by the press as the renaissance of the roadster — that classic English or Italian roadster feeling at an affordable price. At the time, it was one of the lowest-priced sports cars available, making it particularly attractive to women, who made up a large segment of the purchasers. In the Miata, Mazda effectively brought together simplicity, sex appeal, attention to detail, and refinement — all characteristics of a classic design. Incremental design successes followed, and in 1999 Mazda released a model with new contoured headlights and a sleek, muscular body, and it was a runaway success. At the 2005 Geneva Motor Show, the third generation of the Mazda Miata was unveiled.

Tom Matano, one of the Miata's principal designers, attributes the success of the car to its ability to evolve with the changing times and marketplace. He has pointed out that despite many competitors, the MX-5 remained faithful to its original concept as an affordable, two-seat sports car that is fun to drive. It is a feeling shared by many Miata enthusiasts and owners. In addition, Mazda has extended the interface with the car's drivers through its support for the Miata Club, which is managed by and for Miata fans. This creates a feedback mechanism better than any help desk or complaint card.

**Mazda's Designer on "Timeless Design"**

When Miata designer Tom Matano was asked for his opinion on what it is precisely that makes for a "timeless design," he offered the following on the Miata website:

• Timeless/lasting design quality;

• Usefulness;

• Truthfulness, defined as the correct use of materials and technologies, communication of what is "inside" the product, perfect proportions, and an absence of gimmicky lines, forms, and graphics; and

• Technological advancement for its time.

Mazda found a successful approach to understanding the essence of its product, developing designs that maintain the fundamental attributes that made it successful in the first place. But it is the rare product that enjoys a high level of interest over such a long period and with widespread appeal geographically. Most products that reach iconic status do so in a single country, and their appeal lasts for a couple of decades at best. As industry and market competition intensifies and become more dynamic, any long-lived design that significantly reduces the level of product line uncertainty represents a lifeline of stability.

The financial benefits of long-lived designs are obvious. If a design remains viable in the marketplace for a long time, product family sales are likely to be more predictable and the company avoids the costly process of designing replacements for those models. Less apparent is the contribution that classic designs make to simplifying the management of product families. Exhibit 2.1 shows how a few long-lived designs can anchor and stabilize the evolution of a firm's product family by assuring at least a few models that do not require redesign and providing a starting point for the development of other incremental and topological innovations.

It is apparent that successful product families must contain the proper *mix* of model and design longevity. Some customers' needs and preferences will change more rapidly than others. Ideally, companies will offer product

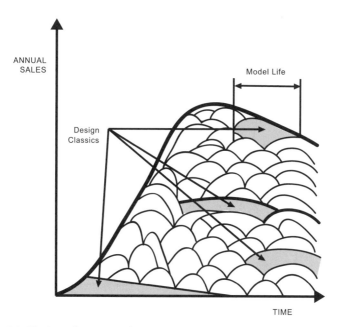

**Exhibit 2.1.** Design classics anchor a product line.

families and models that exactly match those needs. Yet, it is much harder to generate effective long-lived designs than short-lived ones.

**Platform design classics**

Some design classics are designs that survive because they are so excellent that they can become the basis for product architectures or embed key technology. Their longevity typically stems from one of two sources. First, there are situations where competitors cannot change the technology, because it is patented or contains proprietary secrets. Second, there are products where competitors have no incentive to change the design, because they use the same standards. In either case, the product family is likely to resemble Exhibit 2.2.

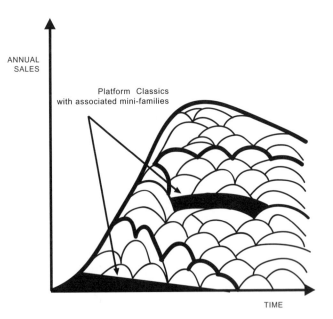

**Exhibit 2.2.** Platform design classics.

A design classic can survive far beyond its closest competitors. Classic designs, though, are far from a sure thing. Technological discontinuities are always a threat. A competitor's design may be selected as the industry standard. At any moment, competitors might succeed in working around a patent, and proprietary secrets may be discovered independently or leak out. To counter these threats, companies apply two complementary approaches to create classic designs. One is new technology — a powerful tool for creating long-lived designs. A proprietary model developed around a new technology often enjoys a period of market leadership. Establishing proprietary ownership of the technology might extend this dominance to a number of incremental variants of a design, and even yield a legal monopoly through patent protection.

Aggressive exploitation by Sony of its new motor, battery, and miniaturization technologies in the Walkman family of products was rewarded in virtually every instance with at least six months' unchallenged leadership of a key market segment. Sony built upon these successes by rapidly embedding each new technology in a number of models that spanned a significant cross section of its market. The company followed this practice successively in CD players, gaming machines, and a variety of other consumer electronics products. Although technology is arguably the most direct and obvious route to a business classic, research suggests that technological advantage, even abetted by patent protection, is increasingly fleeting. Of greater concern is that opportunities for technological improvement are infrequent for most products.

**Proprietary or Open Standards?**

What has been proven *not* to win are proprietary standards. While more complex proprietary standards may produce technical products that are "better," simple and open architectures are what come to dominate markets. The example of videocassette recorders illustrates this point. Sony introduced its Betamax format in 1975, and JVC released the VHS format the next year. The two formats were incompatible, and a standardization rivalry unfolded. No single producer of VCRs had the strength to impose a global standard, so the market took over. Sony kept its format proprietary, while the VHS format was opened, which made possible complementary product alliances. Within a couple of years, the Betamax format — "better" technically — fell behind in market share. Ultimately, Sony ceased production, switching to VHS for the consumer market.[11]

Closely related to the search for new technologies are strategies that revolve around issues of standardization. The lifecycle of a product family that comprises models based on less than state-of-the-art technology can be extended significantly if product designs are aligned with an industry standard, and even further if the manufacturer has been involved in defining or setting the standard.

Several companies (particularly Sony in personal stereos and Toshiba in portable computers) exhibited a product-family evolution from performance to product differentiation. Toshiba's T1100 portable computer and Sony's WMD6C Walkman seemed to be immortal. While an effective design process may have contributed to their longevity, no one in the respective organizations would have predicted the magnitude and durability of their success.

In other situations, customer affection (which can sometimes reach extraordinary levels) can also account for a design's durability. The Colt 45 revolver, still in production 120 years after its introduction, and the Coca Cola bottle, which has remained largely unchanged since 1915 (also reincarnated in larger plastic bottles), come to mind. Neither is state-of-the-art in terms of functionality or manufacturing efficiency. "On occasion," explains Pulos,[12] "a product may be displaced by another that provides the same in a better way in that even the original product will be abandoned. Should it be remembered with affection, however, it may be brought back to be admired as a work of art — a 'classic' absolved of functional responsibility."

Customer affection ranges widely over products and can have many sources. For the Zippo lighter, it is simplicity of design coupled with nostalgia. So beloved was the IBM Selectric by many typists that they would actively resist trying another model. Even the most mundane of products has the potential to elicit such affection; surely a "better" design is possible, yet the Mason jar has been the gold standard for home canning in the United States since 1858.

Customers are frequently reluctant to abandon products that are particularly well matched to their needs, even when newer and objectively better products become available. The Tandy TRS100 portable computer, one of the first offered for sale, illustrates the durability of a well-fitted product. When first introduced in 1983, it had limited memory, a non-standard operating system, and a small display screen. Nevertheless, as other portable computers became available over the next six years that performed better by almost every measure, Tandy continued to enjoy very good sales. What set the TRS100 apart was a unique set of features that made it an ideal portable electronic note taker. Reporters, in particular, fell in love with the TRS100. The computer's full-size keyboard (which accommodated touch typing), extended operation time using conventional batteries, modem compatibility, and price (a few hundred dollars) met their need for a simple, reliable, inexpensive word processor that could be carried anywhere and transmit stories back to the office via telephone. For these users, the spreadsheet and database applications supported by more expensive portable computers were of little consequence.

**Making a strong design statement**

A design classic occasionally results from a designer's use of a product to communicate an abstract idea or vision. A memorable "design statement" that resonates strongly with a group of customers represents the equivalent of a personal conversation between designer and customer. Conversations of this sort accommodate designers' statements on a wide range of issues and topics. Braun's unadorned black-and-white products make statements about simplicity and functionality. Other products make statements about the importance of fun, need for humor or value of freedom, as we shall see in later chapters.

An effective design statement confers substantial advantage on a product. Customers sympathetic to the statement are likely to purchase a product and the transactions, because the implicit dialog is built around shared values, are likely to be intense and mutually rewarding. Other parties tend to find it difficult to interrupt such a conversation.

Although well understood by designers, this aspect of design poses a challenge for managers of commercial innovation. Design statements are value judgments; a perceptive designer can identify a market segment that shares a particular view. Appreciation for a designer's vision might come less readily to a multi-faceted organization, however, and many managers are uncomfortable with the notion of their designers engaging directly in conversations with customers. Management interruption of a designer-customer dialog, even if justified by other business considerations, inevitably weakens a design statement. In light of this, companies able to sustain a distinctive design statement in all their products — Braun, Sony, and Apple Computer, among others — have surely achieved something noteworthy.

Strong, consistent and persistent design statements tend to emanate from organizations that have either an outstanding lead designer or a particularly perceptive leader. In firms that lack these human resources, design statements are often ineffective or, more likely, the company as a whole is unable to sustain a coherent customer dialog.

A record of memorable designs usually reflects commitment to the creative aspects of product design. The most successful firms in this regard are those that attach considerable value to the skills of industrial designers. They encourage their designers to take maximum advantage of an atmosphere of free design thinking in the firm. Long-lived designs often succeed precisely because they violate conventional assumptions and redefine customer expectations. Companies that must bet on their designers' judgment must be willing to recruit design staff that possess skills that inspire confidence.

The variety-driven approach to product planning seems particularly well suited to the development of business classics. Exhibit 2.3 plots the survival curves for four major manufacturers' US models. The average life of Sony's models was nearly twice that of its competitors, from which it could be construed that Sony is a sluggish innovator. Yet the company is widely regarded as being highly innovative and its large market share suggests that it has managed to maintain relevance with customers.

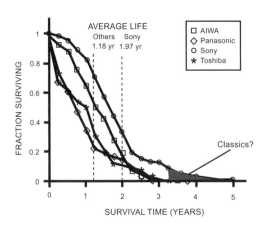

**Exhibit 2.3.** Survival curves for personal portable stereos (1980–1989).

Many of Sony's long-lived models in the upper tail of the survival curve qualify as business classics. So well adapted were these designs to the needs of their target customers that Sony encountered little market pressure to redesign them. Consider the WMF45 Sports Walkman design, which possessed little in the way of new technology and, being radical for its time, made no appeal to nostalgia. Although clearly a product of creative designers, Sony's expectations for the design were initially limited. Intended to be a regional design for the US market, the model was not included in the company's Japanese product line. Yet the Sports Walkman not only virtually owned the US market for active lifestyles portable music for nearly the entire period prior to the introduction of the MP3 player, it also spawned a large family of horizontal classics that range from CD players to video camcorders — all from an incremental design.

Eventually, Sony's portable music players did lose a significant degree of their appeal in the market, largely because the company made a strategic error in where it focused improvements. Sony worked to improve what had been the traditional performance criterion for a personal music player — sound quality — and developed its Discman to play CDs at a high level of sound performance. A new technology came along, however, and MP3 players (with their compressed sound quality) demonstrated that the old criterion was no longer the consumer market's main criterion.

**Apple's iPod**

Apple Computer's iPod (Exhibit 2.4) is one of the more outstanding designs of a consumer product in recent memory. In many ways, it is

Mini    Nano    Shuffle

**Exhibit 2.4.** The iPod family of MP3 players.

the epitome of the main points we made in Chapter 1 when we defined design-inspired innovation. The iPod delights its customers with the simplicity and elegance of its design. It seamlessly integrates the hardware and service components of Apple's offering. And there is no denying that it has generated emotional and symbolic value among the product users.

Initially conceived of primarily as a digital "version" of the Sony Walkman, the iPod — released in October 2001 — is a pocket-size, portable digital MP3 audio player with a simple user interface designed around a central scroll wheel (the "Apple Click Wheel"). Most iPod models store media on built-in memory and, like most digital audio players, an iPod connected to a computer can serve as an external data storage device.

The iPod is a stellar example of what Christensen calls a "disruptive innovation" (after coining the term "disruptive technology", he later replaced it in recognition of the fact that few *technologies* are intrinsically disruptive, but rather that strategy creates a disruptive impact).[13] Innovating on the platform of the new MP3 technology invented elsewhere, Apple created a product and service that overturns the existing standard in the market. A disruptive technology comes to the fore by fulfilling a role in a new market that the older technology could not fill (a good example being smaller-size hard drives, which made notebook computers possible in the 1980s) and through successive performance improvements that change the landscape of performance criteria and displace market incumbents (as digital photography has come to replace film photography).

It is important to reiterate that the iPod was not the first of its kind. In fact, the first product representing an innovation is rarely the one that becomes the design classic. There is almost always a period of user experimentation before the market settles for the enduring leader.

The importance of disruptive innovation is not primarily that a dominant design is ultimately overturned. Rather, it is that it broadens the definition of a product category, and this may dramatically expand the market. Research has shown that innovations such as incandescent lighting, machine-made ice, and film photography each expanded their respective market by an order of magnitude or more.[14] Christensen fully documents this phenomenon for computer hard disc drives. Innovations are disruptive not because they provide superior function conventionally measured; often, they do not — as in the example of MP3 data compression, which provides an inferior sound quality when compared with music on a magnetic tape or compact disc.[15] Instead, to be disruptive an innovation must provide a different and broader functionality.

In the case of the MP3 player, broader functionality means having a thousand songs in one's pocket rather than just a dozen on a tape cassette. People who would have never considered buying a Walkman were avid about trying the iPod. Ultimately, disruptive innovations make the function they provide inexpensive and convenient, playing into powerfully elastic demand. So today we take for granted that we can switch on the light to read, gaze out of large clear windows, take a cold beverage from the refrigerator, or appreciate a photograph on our laptop computer. Why would we mourn the demise of dangerous, smoky gas lamps or lament the passing of the ice-man or the floppy disc as being disrupted? These were comparatively costly, inconvenient, and not so widely available.

## The Dominance of the iPod

To say that iPod has dominated the U.S. digital music player market seems like an understatement. Apple has sold more than 15 million in less than four years. Figures from October 2004 indicate that the Apple product enjoyed more than 90 percent of the market for hard-drive based MP3 players and more than 70 percent of the market for all types of MP3 players. Thanks in large part to the iPod, Apple announced for its fiscal 2005 fourth quarter the highest revenue and earnings in the company's history. The figures represented a 200 percent growth in iPods over the same quarter of the previous year. In addition, there was a 48 percent growth in Macintosh computers — perhaps an indication of what Apple calls the "halo effect" that encourages iPod users to switch to other Apple products. Results for the first two quarters of 2006 were similarly impressive.

Several things about the iPod set it apart from the competition. One, of course, is its portability and ease of use. Another is that more than a physical product, the iPod comes with a fully integrated service and user interface: namely, the iTunes media library software. iTunes allows users to manage their own music libraries on the iPod and on their computers and includes an online store for purchasing digital music. With iTunes, a user can automatically synchronize her iPod with specific playlists or with the entire contents of a music library whenever the iPod is connected to a host computer. In fact, the iPod allows the user — as Steve Jobs, Apple's CEO, puts it — "to put your entire music collection in your pocket and listen to it wherever you go."

When first released, the iPod was only compatible with Macintosh computers. Later, Apple added Windows compatibility, opening the technology so iTunes can be run on any computer, allowing the synergy between the iPod and iTunes to be accessed by all users. Open standards are in line with Apple's turn to *encouraging* innovation with its products. Open standards create the space for hundreds of partners to help drive profits and growth. By incorporating expansion slots in its early Apple II computer, other companies were encouraged to develop disk drives, number tablets, and specialized circuit cards and other accessories. As a result Apple took only nine years to enter the Fortune 500 list of largest companies, cutting Ford's previous record by nearly half. Later, Apple shifted strategy with its Macintosh, seeking a perfect, optimized design. The company tried to drive all the value itself, while the competing PC could be cloned (and hence had a more attractive price). Apple became a less significant player. The shift back to an open approach with the iPod has had results as dramatic and positive for the company as those realized from the Apple II. The outpouring of accessories and added applications that have resulted parallels the dynamic of Apple's early success.

The user interface for both the product and the service encourages innovation, and the product has created a tremendous desire among users to create new and expanded uses for the iPod. Companies are being formed around the iPod, which has created a large and growing aftermarket accessory industry — what Steve Jobs referred to in his keynote address at the 2005 Macworld as "the iPod economy" (and that some others have called "the iPod ecology"). The availability of these aftermarket products surely creates some of iPod's popularity among consumers. The device can also display notes and host simple games. iPod accessories include FM tuners, memory-card readers, voice recording modules, and speaker systems. The Bose speaker system, and others since its introduction, uses the docking connectors at the iPod's bottom.

## The iPod Design Chain

How Apple came to develop the iPod is a story worth telling. Much of the underlying design was done outside the company. Apple partnered with PortalPlayer, a California-based developer with design expertise in portable music devices. PortalPlayer then chose other partners and managed the process. Erik Sherman[16] writes of a design "from the outside in" — Apple "had a vision of what the player should be and what it would look like. The subsequent design parameters were dictated by its appearance and form factor."

Apple's five key partners for the iPod are Sony (battery), Wolfson (Codec and digital-to-analog converter), Toshiba (disk drive), Texas Instruments (FireWire technology), and Linear Technology (power management). Working with these components, PortalPlayer was able to develop a reference model for a high-quality player. Notably, the design chain relied on *off-the-shelf* components, but they were integrated with elegance.

Sherman notes that "it would be a huge mistake to assume that all the design work happened elsewhere and that Apple had no substantial input." Where Apple added its own value was in "putting it all together and optimizing the design to eke out the best performance ..." The user interface, perhaps the product's greatest achievement, is all Apple.

The innovations with the iPod, which continue unabated, include relatively minor features such as the iBeam that turns the iPod into a flashlight or laser pointer and more complex advances that turn the iPod into a camera and a phone. A visual presentation may be stored in an iPod and projected directly from a digital projector. Accessories such as external speakers and a Bluetooth gizmo make it possible to broadcast the iPod through a car radio. In Summer 2004, the German carmaker BMW started selling an iPod connector for four of its most popular models and now others, such as Volvo, are following suit. The connector allows drivers to control their iPods using buttons on their radio or steering wheel.

One of the most significant innovations related to the iPod is podcasting technology, a method of publishing audio and video programs via the Internet that allows automatic downloading onto portable players or personal computers. A feed delivers an enclosed file to the user's device. Users may subscribe to feeds using so-called podcatching" software that periodically — and automatically — checks for and downloads new content, making it possible for people to take podcasts with them on their MP3 players and listen to them whenever they want.

Increasingly, traditional broadcasters are adopting the podcasting format. Seattle's news radio station KOMO regularly distributes its news programs through podcasting. WGBH in Boston offers podcasts of many of its regular programs. A growing number of National Public Radio stations in the United States podcast their productions. In March 2005,

Virgin Radio began to produce a daily podcast of its popular morning drive time show. The BBC announced in April 2005 that it would extend its podcasting trial to include close to 25 programs.

Apple's own active involvement with the technology that takes its name, in part, from an Apple product began only in mid-2005. The company became a source of "podcatcher" software and started to provide tutorials on how to create podcasts using Apple products Quicktime Pro and Garage Band. Most notably, for our discussion, is that Apple added a podcast-subscription feature to its late June 2005 release of iTunes 4.9, and launched a directory of podcasts — initially, some 3,000 entries — at the iTunes Music Store. In doing so, Apple strengthened the fully integrated service and user interface of its product.

The iPod offers a model for the future, where open standards prevail. The iPod is a disruptive innovation that draws in new players. The innovations possible on the iPod platform are too numerous to imagine for most of us. With its beautiful user interface, it is destined to become a design classic.

**The challenge for the future**

A design classic such as the Volkswagen Beetle is an example of a prevailing design, one that stays attractive for a very long time, while being thoroughly transformed under the hood. We might even call it *iconic*. This is a lesson underscored by the Walkman story. The iPod is the same: Apple did not stay just with the initial hard disc technology, but opted for a supplementary range of flash memory iPods. With the introduction of the iPod Nano, Apple created further buzz, pointing to another lesson superbly illustrated by the Walkman case: the power of creating a family of products all identified as belonging to the same design classic cohort.

Some product designs become so established and so indistinguishable as to become almost commodities. Consider the ordinary bicycle. Many people buy one just for its height, even without the gearshift option. In such a category, the premium value is to stand out and design for some particular function, such as the mountain bike. This is decidedly up-market and offers numerous possibilities for product differentiation (e.g., front and rear cushioning). One real winner would seem to be Shimano, producer of the transmission that offers a choice between different numbers of gears. Shimano so dominates as the designer that bicycle producers emphasize that they offer "true" Shimano gears. Thus, out of a bland category arises a product that seems drastically differentiated from the run of the mill.

As mentioned previously, the rule seems almost to be that the leader during one generation of technology dwells too long and gets caught napping by a competitor for the next generation. Two Japanese companies have played this flip-flop game for memory chips, and despite being aware of the race, they seem incapable of figuring out how to transcend their initial successes to *keep* winning. Apple, with the iPod, seems to be aware of this temptation to rest on one's laurels.

Psychologists tell us that we tend to feel comfortable with an idea that is "good enough," and then we stop searching for alternatives. A

Scandinavian producer of heavy equipment for the paper and pulp industry was the uncontested leader for a major type of machinery it had invented. Suddenly, the market eroded because a competitor introduced a much superior product. What galled the loser was that the competition relied upon old technology — the breakthrough had nothing to do with new knowledge, technology, or the progress of science. The "raw material" for the new solution had been there all along, for decades. Later in the book, we will get more clues to how industrial designers may assist in generating profound new options.

To be successful, designers must develop an acute sense for what is "contemporary," what is likely to catch on. Once Apple, which did not invent the translucent look for computers, introduced it in its products (even the cabling), this stylistic element caught on rapidly for the most diverse products — including shavers. Apple set a trend. The original Macintosh was an offshoot of Xerox PARC's Alto system, which took more than a little from what Doug Engelbart had developed earlier at SRI International. Later, the Mac interface was emulated in Windows. We hailed Raymond Loewy's Studebaker as a classic design, despite no runaway sales success, because so many of its elements can be seen in the more successful competing car models that were thoroughly influenced by the pioneer. These succeeding cars were more to the taste of the general public, just as Apple with the iPod took someone else's idea and made something more meaningful of it.

Designers are certainly not infallible soothsayers, or they would find their doors beaten in. Italian star designer Michele De Lucchi confesses to being clueless: one of his designs that he did not think much of turned out to be a huge bestseller, while another he loved bombed in the market. There is no surefire prescription for innovation and none for creating design classics: perhaps such a recipe would be self-defeating. As Caves has underlined, nobody knows for sure about innovation and design success.[17]

Even apart from all these arguments, we suspect that leaders already intuitively understand the contribution design classics can make to a firm's success.

How, then, do companies achieve excellence and elegance in design? We find the answer, in part, in the ways in which companies organize their design functions. To understand that, we develop in the following chapters a clearer understanding of just what *design* means and the processes through which winning product designs are created.

### Endnotes

[1]K.B. Clark and T. Fujimoto, 1991; R.A. Cooper and M. Press, 1995; R.M. Henderson and K.B. Clark, 1990; E.M. Rogers, 1995.
[2]J.M. Utterback and W.J. Abernathy, 1975; W.J. Abernathy and J.M. Utterback, 1978.
[3]M.A. Maidique and B.J. Zirger, 1985.
[4]E. von Hippel, 1988.
[5]Henderson and Clark, 1990.
[6]C.M. Christensen, 1997.
[7]E. von Hippel, 2005.
[8]S. Sanderson and V. Uzumeri, 1997.
[9]W.J. Abernathy and K.B. Clark, 1985.
[10]J.K. Yamaguchi, J. Thompson, and H. Tajima, 1989.
[11]M. Cusumano, Y. Mylonadis, and R. Rosenbloom, 1992.
[12]A.J. Pulos, 1983.

[13]Christensen, 1997.

[14]J.M. Utterback, 1994.

[15]Christensen states that a disruptive technology is always inferior in perfomance, as defined using traditional measures. However, this does not stand up to careful examination of sampled instances. See for example, J.M. Utterback and H.J. Acee, 2005.

[16]E. Sherman, 2002.

[17]R.E. Caves, 2000.

# Chapter 3

# *INTEGRATING FUNCTION AND DESIGN*

The divergent cases of the Sony Walkman and the Apple iPod reflect and epitomize the broader changes we perceive to be occurring with products and innovation. Sony laboriously developed the Walkman — primarily a piece of hardware or an artifact — around its required components and functions, including miniature motors, tape transport and reading heads, and earphones. Designers were employed to develop the product's topology and form for different market segments: sports, children, commuters and so on.

Contrast the iPod, which has been said to represent "an ecology of innovation" or an "iPod economy." Apple developed neither the compression format nor the basic components for its product. Rather, designers were involved from the outset to devise the overall integration of the product and user experience as well as its form. The iPod is not simply hardware that plays music, but rather is a complex of software, services, subscription offerings such as video, user-developed ideas such as podcasting, and various accessories and partnerships. This is exemplified by the partnership announced, as we write, between Apple and Nike. Sensors and a wireless device will be added to some of Nike's running shoes, and the runner's performance will be broadcast to his or her iPod. The iPod may then respond by playing appropriate motivational music to improve the runner's pace. When the device is next synchronized, data will automatically be sent to Nike's website where customers can check their training progress.[1] The variations and themes that might be developed in this manner seem almost endless.

Both the iPod and the Walkman are exemplars of what we defined in Chapter 2 as long-lived design classics. But the iPod goes far beyond excellence in function to be an exemplar of design-inspired innovation. The product illustrates how the boundaries of form and function are becoming blurred or, perhaps more accurately, are intersecting. The boundaries between product as hardware or artifact and software and services are similarly blurred. Few products today function well on their own, nor are many services delivered without intensive use of hardware and software. Both are increasingly defined by their users' participation and adaptation. Truly, "an ecology of innovation" may be the apt term for what is unfolding.

Once a dominant design emerges, product differentiation around that design becomes the most important dynamic of innovation. Technological innovation gives way to simpler, more elegant product design.[2]

**What is "design"? What is research and development?**

Design activities are difficult to define and have a complex relationship with both technological innovation and research and development. In English, the word *design* — like the word *innovation* — refers both to a process and the outcome of a process, which only makes the challenge of defining it more difficult. To understand what design is also requires a clear picture of what constitutes R&D, since R&D is widely conceived to play the central role in the innovation process. The OECD, for instance, officially identifies three activities under the rubric of R&D: basic research, applied research, and experimental development.

In the industrial arena, the vast majority of design work is geared towards production processes. As such, it is not classified as research and development. Nevertheless, some elements of design work *are* R&D, including designs and drawings to define procedures, technical specifications, and operational features needed to conceive, develop, and manufacture new products and processes.

Design, though, is much broader than is R&D. As Walsh[3] points out, "all products are designed, from clothes to engineering components, from magazines to consumer electronics, from kitchen gadgets to chemical plants, from advertisements to salesroom interiors." Conversely, not all products are the immediate consequence of R&D. Design, according to Walsh, is both the process — the series of decisions about the form and function of products, plus decisions about the mode of production and perhaps even delivery — and the outcome of that process, the product itself. As a process, designing is not confined only to solving narrow technological problems.

Consider Exhibit 3.1, which shows how design (D) and R&D (R) relate in terms of their relative size and overlap. We consider the relationship to be best represented by the sets on the middle right of the diagram.

### Scholarly Study of Design versus R&D

Scholars of innovation have largely neglected design activities,[4] emphasizing functional novelty in their focus on technological innovation. Research and development are seen as the primary sources of functionally new technologies, and the sectors of choice for detailed examination have long tended to be those that devote a higher-than-average share of their resources (employees and/or revenues) to R&D, and that tend to have higher-than-average rates of patenting (biotechnology, pharmaceuticals, chemicals, aerospace, and so on).[5] By contrast, as Walsh writes, "Design ... has been far less thoroughly studied from a social science perspective than innovation or R&D."[6]

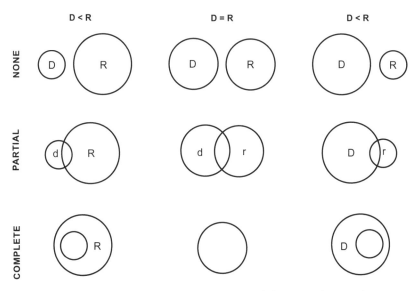

Exhibit 3.1. Relative size and degree of overlap of design and research.

The fact that designers are not always the ones who engage in design activities is one reason design is so hard to identify. What Gorb and Dumas call "silent design" is widespread. For instance, among the British firms that won a Millennium Products award for introducing an exemplarily "well-designed product," 19 percent indicated in a survey that the product development included neither an internal designer, internal design team, or external specialist designer. Nevertheless, these products were *designed* — albeit without the input of a professional designer.[7]

Organizational structures reflect the different understandings firms have of "design." Some see it narrowly as aesthetics, styling, "fitness for use," or performance. These firms are more likely to engage in "silent design" (or see design as part of another function). Other firms take a much broader view, adding to the narrow list efficiency in production and use of materials, safety or durability, and so on. They are more likely to be design-focused or even design-led. Notably, there is a positive association between better commercial performance and interpreting design broadly rather than narrowly.[8]

### Design, Innovation, and the Boundaries of the Firm

Vivien Walsh, in her 1996 paper "Design, innovation and the boundaries of the firm," explains that design activities overlap with both R&D and technological innovation, but also can contribute to a firm's business beyond these categories. Further, she observes that design "does not fit easily within either the [firm's] internal or external boundaries," and notes that design's location within firms often varies "with different national cultures and traditions; in R&D, production and marketing as well as in specialist design and development departments; and increasingly often, outside the manufacturing firm in design consultancy firms."

Within firms, Walsh observes a particular division between engineering and other design disciplines, and even between engineering and industrial design — "which are both concerned with different facets of the design of products and artifacts." Organizational diffuseness of design as an activity makes it "very easy to overlook design and not take it into account adequately in the development of strategies" for the firm's success. We discuss the concept of *integrated design* in later chapters.

Design relates to a number of activities and disciplines, some of which draw heavily on artistic capabilities and others of which are closely connected to engineering (and, to a lesser degree, science). Part of what makes design interesting is the creative combination of the artistic and engineering/scientific elements. Fundamentally, design "involves the *creative visualization* of concepts, plans and ideas" (as Walsh emphasizes).[9] As a process, as opposed to an outcome, design is first and foremost cognitive. The design process employs tools such as sketches, blueprints, and models, but while these tools are typical of design activities, they are not the process itself. We will note in later chapters the importance of the uses of sketches, models, and other visual tools in designs.

Exhibit 3.2 attempts to position various types of design activities in two dimensions. On one dimension, the extent to which the activity draws on engineering/scientific inputs or capabilities is distinguished from the extent to which it draws on artistic inputs. The second dimension distinguishes the nature of the outputs from wholly material products (with little or no symbolic value) to wholly symbolic products (with little or no material existence). Nearly all products or product systems are a mixture.

Innovation studies have focused heavily on the highly functional activities in the bottom right of Exhibit 3.2. Shifting the focus to product design activities brings us nearer to the center of the figure's space, where

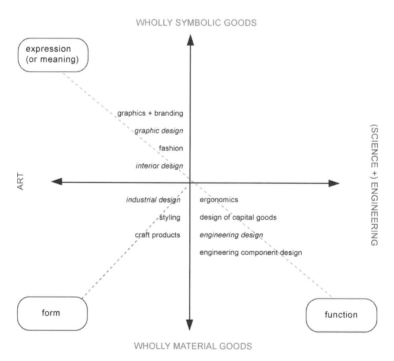

**Exhibit 3.2.** Engineering and artistic input of design activities.

we can explore *industrial* design and its interrelationship with *engineering* design.[10] All manufactured products (and the majority of services) have been designed, formally or informally, poorly or well, but industrial and engineering design are essentially the two types of design activity most directly relevant to industrial products.

### Concrete Canvas

Millions of people live in areas affected by natural disasters and civil wars, and providing shelter for them is no easy task. A radical design innovation by Peter Brewin and Will Crawford, two postgraduate students at the Royal College of Art in London, aims to change the situation.

The pair began not with the problem, but with a desire to work with a material that interested them: concrete. They had heard about inflatable structures that can be built around broken gas pipes to do repairs safely, and wondered about an inflatable concrete shelter. "This gave us the idea of making a giant concrete eggshell for a shelter, using inflation to optimize the structure," says Brewin. "Eggs are structures with enormous strength for a very thin wall."

After a month in Uganda investigating the specific conditions in which the shelters would be used, Brewin and Crawford knew their structure would have to be extremely easy to assemble and able to withstand hostile environments. Dubbed Concrete Canvas, their shelter is made from a plastic liner covered with a cement-impregnated fabric. The assembler literally adds some water and presses a button to inflate the plastic liner. After 12 hours, the 12-millimeter-thick (less than half an inch) shell solidifies. Full-scale models, once produced, will have 52.4 square meters (172 square feet) of floor space, weigh about 500 pounds (230 kg), and should last for 10 years.

Concrete Canvas is an attractive alternative to tents and pre-fabricated buildings — the predominant approaches to emergency shelter. It is almost as easy to transport as a tent, but is as durable and secure as a prefabricated building. It can be covered with sand or earth to improve insulation and can be demolished fairly easily with little rubble. The shelter can even be supplied sterile for medical purposes.

Brewin and Crawford's idea and prototype have won several design awards, and they established a company, Crawford Brewin Ltd., to bring the concept to market.

These two types of design are quite distinct and have different perspectives. The creative activity of industrial design aims to determine the formal qualities of objects produced by industry. Maldonado notes that although these formal qualities include aesthetics, which is the aspect most commonly associated with design in everyday language, they "are principally those structural and functional relationships which convert a system into a coherent unity from the point of view of both the producer and the user."[11] Industrial design relates significantly to how the functionality of a product is delivered to the user. Engineering design, by contrast, uses scientific principles, technical information, and the imagination to define a mechanical structure, machine, or system to perform specified functions with the maximum economy and efficiency.

Both industrial and engineering design are applied to industrial products, although to varying degrees. Tensions can arise between the two because they have quite different approaches and perspectives despite both activities' concern with contextual issues such as product performance and the relationship between performance and price ("value-for-money").

Design, particularly industrial design, is often concerned with making a product "transparent" and its functional architecture "invisible." In other words, the user should be able to use the product with ease without needing to know how the product does what it does.[12] The industrial designer must understand the user's perspective, while a design engineer may be more concerned with the objective characteristics of the technology.[13] Engineering design is often formally organized and is most likely to be included in R&D.

Regardless of their size or industry, some companies devote more resources to formal industrial design activities. Others pay scant attention. Moody uses the analogy of architecture: "Industrial design is to engineering as architecture is to building. Machinery and equipment can be devised without the aid of an industrial designer, just as buildings can be devised without the aid of architects."[14] It does not require industrial design *training* to do industrial design — and hence we have "silent design" in which marketing, production, and other staff contribute to design decisions, or are involved in the design and development work, even though they are not officially designated as "designers."

In some companies, industrial design is the last stage of product development, when the final styling is added to make the products acceptable for the market. This is "form following function" or "designing from the inside out," as opposed to "function following form" or "designing from the outside in," which is when industrial designers set the parameters within which products are developed.[15] These different approaches often reflect different interpretations of the purpose of design (and different locations of the design function within firms). For instance, marketing staff and marketing-led firms commonly think of design as the means by which products are made distinct, tempting consumers to buy and making it easier for marketing to distinguish the firm's products from those of its rivals.[16]

Design's purpose, though, goes well beyond aesthetics. As the Design Council indicates, it is "the process through which technical ability is focused on customer needs in terms of performance, human factors, appearance, and value for money."[18] This, though, is easier said than done, because the designer stands at the interface between the producer and the user, so his or her knowledge of the latter in particular will always be incomplete. Ideally, in creating a new product, the designer seeks to understand not only the user's formal needs but also the user's preconceptions and prejudices. Good design, says Moody, is "a continuous extension of the user," whereas poor design is "psychologically incompatible" with users' preconceptions and behavior.[18]

### When Design Focuses — and Fails to Focus — On User Needs

Many writers on design emphasize the focus on customer or user needs. Pugh's first principle of "Total Design" is that "the user need/customer requirement/voice of the customer is paramount to the success or failure of the product."[19] For Freeman, design plays the vital role of "coupling" user needs with technical possibilities.[20] Archer sees it as "the trick of discovering which set of attributes prospective purchasers would value and of discovering a product configuration embodying them at the right price."[21] Finally, Walsh *et al.* describe design as "the vital link between a market need, an invention or innovative idea and its translation into a product suitable for manufacture and use."[22]

Whether industrial or engineering design in industry, the collective purpose is to deliver to the user the utility (or functionality) of a product in a manner fully compatible with that user's requirements (including cost considerations). Often, though, designers simply claim to "know" what users want, or they assume that users want what the designer would want.[23] They end up ignoring the user. The myriad products that are awkward for left-handed people to use are a striking example. The designers — most likely right-handed — of products from potato peelers to photocopiers rarely notice or are aware of the inconvenience of these products to left-handers.

Contrast this with OXO International, "dedicated to providing innovative consumer products that make everyday living easier." The company produces a line of kitchen utensils that feature big, soft handles that accommodate, for example, the growing market segment of senior citizens whose ability to hold an item firmly has diminished in an age-weakened hand. The products reflect OXO's "universal design" philosophy of "making products that are easy to use for the widest possible spectrum of users."

Effective designs evolve, explains Rothwell: with each generation, the product is refined to suit better users' needs, behavior, and idiosyncrasies.[24] Over the same period, users may grow so accustomed to a design that it enters the psyche and comes to be considered *the* "natural" design — as is the case with some "dominant designs."[25] For example, when the battle tank was first invented, attempts were made to make it walk (like an insect) and burrow (like a mole). Today, the thought of a walking, burrowing tank seems the stuff of science fiction. We all "know" a tank is a tracked vehicle with a gun mounted in a turret — despite the fact that there is nothing "natural" or inevitable about this established form.

### Design as a Milestone of Change

Design is a milestone of change when a dominant new product emerges that represents the synthesis of individual technological innovations that were introduced independently in prior products. Dominant design enforces standards, allows for economies in production, and then opens competition on the basis of cost as well as product performance.

Some product design milestones from the past include sealed refrigeration units for home refrigerators and freezers, effective can-sealing technology in the food canning industry, and the standard diesel locomotive in the railroad industry.[26] In each case, the milestone signals a significant transformation, affecting the type of innovation that follows, the source of information, and the size, scope, and use of formal research and development.

Others, such as Pinch and Bijker, have argued that dominant product design is socially constructed and conceptually bounded, and that the process of design is intrinsically linked to the preconceptions and prejudices of both the users and the designer.[27] Apple's iPod, presented in Chapter 2, is an example of a design rapidly becoming dominant. It is one that melds these ideas of technological innovation and social construction to create a self-reinforcing system in which the user desires the ever-expanding "package" represented by the physical iPod, accessories, and the attendant services.

In general, design is not about the creation or use of "new technology" in a narrow sense, and it is certainly not about the creation or use of new technologies for their own sake, although design activities can lead to the creation or use of new technologies. The point is that technological innovation is partially about the development of new technologies, in the narrow sense of building technical novelty into products, but it is also about the creation and incorporation of new or significantly altered concepts and ideas. The deeply embedded understandings that both designers and users come to associate with products can make us very conservative. For example, one Design Award-winning company introduced a fiber-reinforced plastic tanker truck, which had some significant advantages (in terms of safety) over existing metal tankers, but did not succeed in the marketplace. Asked how the companies' competitors had responded to this innovation, the firm wrote, "With the belief that new technology would not succeed due to the entrenched idea that only metal tankers were suitable. They were right!"

Similarly, but on the production side, James Dyson — inventor of the bagless vacuum cleaner that is now Britain's market leader — could not persuade an existing manufacturer to produce the product. Again, when LEGO® was offered the concept of K'NEX, a toy system idea similar to LEGO, they rejected it — and today K'NEX is one of the significant competitors of LEGO.

### James Dyson and the Bagless Vacuum Cleaner

James Dyson's "dual cyclone" vacuum cleaner provides an interesting illustration of design-based innovation. A designer trained at the Royal College of Art in London, Dyson grew dissatisfied with the rapid deterioration in suction with "bag" vacuum cleaners as it got clogged. He identified the problem as caused by the increased thickness of the dust in the walls of the bag, which reduces suction and therefore the effectiveness of the cleaner. Inspired by the use of cyclones to extract dust from sawmills, he set out in 1978 — with no theoretical knowledge of the physics of cyclones and no engineering background — to develop a "bagless" vacuum cleaner.

Dyson believes that one learns significantly from making mistakes and then improvements, which he believes should be done quickly and inexpensively. In designing his vacuum, he used quick prototypes made of cardboard, devising and testing more than 5,000. His approach exemplifies the "seeking and experimenting" described in Chapter 1.

Five years later, Dyson had an effective prototype, obtained some patents to protect his idea, and set out to license his design (see Exhibit 3.3) to existing vacuum cleaner manufacturers, including Hoover and Electrolux. He was unable to reach an agreement with these producers. One suggestion for why is that he sought too high a royalty, but it is clear that the incumbents employed a "razor-blade" marketing model in which most money was made not from the initial sale of the cleaner but from the subsequent purchase of consumables such as replacement bags. Hence, they were not keen to take up Dyson's invention. The effect was to compel Dyson to go into production himself, which he began, at considerable risk, in 1992. He did not know whether

**Exhibit 3.3.** Dyson products.

consumers shared his dissatisfaction with the bag vacuum cleaner or whether they would be willing to pay a premium for a bagless version. Nor could he anticipate how the incumbents might react. (Hoover subsequently stated that they wished they had licensed Dyson's invention in order to bury the product.)[28] Additionally, venture capitalists did not like the fact that the product was a vacuum, nor that the founder of the firm was a designer and not an engineer. As a result, manufacturing began with minimal funding — just enough for tooling in a borrowed factory.

With his designer skills, Dyson placed a strong emphasis on the quality and styling of his product, making it more desirable than most existing vacuum cleaners. He ignored marketing research and made the machine transparent because *he* found that intriguing. He focused on customer service that would help him learn about any weaknesses in the product and enhance the young company's reputation with consumers, whose direct recommendations to others would be more powerful than any advertising. Another innovation was putting the help-line phone number on the product itself. A user who has a problem simply dials the number on a cellular phone, places the phone on the machine, and the motor signal and its serial number are transmitted to the company. This often allows a remote diagnosis of the problem. From the serial number, the company also knows the user's address and thus who might best respond to provide help.

In the market, Dyson benefited from Hoover's "free flights" marketing fiasco of 1992–1993,[29] which damaged the reputation of a key incumbent. Two of the largest and most prominent UK electrical chains, Comet and Curry's, endorsed the Dyson product by agreeing to offer it in their stores. This helped boost the brand. Even though Dyson sold his vacuum for two or three times the price of competitive models, the company still enjoyed rapid market penetration. Within two-and-a-half years, Dyson was the largest selling vacuum in Britain.

Today, Dyson's success has changed the industry. A large number of new entrants have followed Dyson with "me-too" bagless vacuum cleaners. Meanwhile, Dyson has continued to innovate, introducing new and enhanced products over the past decade. He sticks to his view that encouraging creativity is entirely a matter of how one behaves. Never be cynical about ideas that seem silly — like putting the help number on top of each machine. Don't ridicule those ideas. Encourage the mistakes that lead to learning.

### The growth of outside design services

In recent years, there has been significant growth in the purchase of design services by firms in the United Kingdom and other countries. According to the British Design Initiative/Design Council "Design Industry Valuation Survey," in 2002 there were about 3,700 companies working in the UK design consultancy sector, with revenue of almost $11 billion (£6 billion) and employing some 67,000 people.[30] Comparison with several earlier studies suggests that these figures have been growing since at least the mid-1980s.[31]

The rapid growth in design consulting over recent years points to an increasing separation of design activities from production activities. This separation suggests considerable value added in the practice of design that may, indeed, exceed that from production. It also suggests a shift away from the traditional model of innovation in which the design or broader new product development function is embedded in the firm as part of the wider set of production processes.[32]

A range of arrangements is possible (Exhibit 3.4). Firms may contract their design requirements to consultants. Alternatively, principal firms

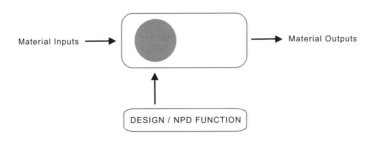

Traditional Model of New Product Development (NPD) Embedded within Manufacturing

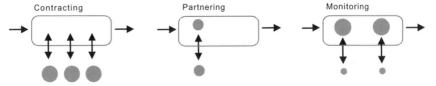

The Range of New Arrangements

**Exhibit 3.4.** Changing relationship between principal firms and design consultancies.

may retain a significant design capability but partner with one or more design consultants to develop new products or services. A third possibility is monitoring: the principal essentially retains the capability to design new products or services but uses one or more consultants to monitor wider trends.

In all of these different configurations we should ask what is gained and what is lost, which in turn raises questions about how design and new product development can be most effectively managed. Although in Exhibit 3.4 the manufacturer initially contracts design activities to a consultant, conceivably the relationship is reversed, with the design consultant effectively arranging for contract manufacturing.[33]

Exhibit 3.5 shows the regional distribution and size of firms engaged in engineering design and consulting, and product design consulting in the United Kingdom. The data indicate that design consultancies are predominately small operations, and that they cluster together.[34]

| Employment Size | Product Design | | | Engineering Design | | |
|---|---|---|---|---|---|---|
| | London | East & South East | Other Regions | London | East & South East | Other Regions |
| 0 to 5 | 48% | 60% | 60% | 47% | 62% | 57% |
| 6 to 10 | 18% | 16% | 14% | 15% | 12% | 15% |
| 11 to 20 | 14% | 7% | 9% | 12% | 6% | 11% |
| 21 to 50 | 9% | 11% | 7% | 9% | 10% | 7% |
| 51+ | 11% | 6% | 9% | 18% | 11% | 10% |
| All | 100% | 100% | 100% | 100% | 100% | 100% |
| % of Firms | 37% | 28% | 35% | 17% | 42% | 41% |
| % of Employment | 40% | 26% | 33% | 21% | 42% | 37% |

*Source:* British Design Initiative database.

**Exhibit 3.5.** Regional distribution and size of UK product and engineering design consultancies.

One thing Exhibit 3.5 does not show concerns how these operations are changing over time. For instance, designers can develop new product ideas from scratch or may simply adapt existing products to local markets. In some cases, they are engaged solely to generate ideas that are not even intended for production.[35] Further, Exhibit 3.5 offers no explanation for why similar firms, in this case design firms, seem to cluster together.

### Red-Eye Intravenous Drip Monitor

George Gallagher never imagined that a visit to his sick wife in the hospital would spur him to create a product and win the BBC Tomorrow's World Health Innovation Award in 2001. His wife Jenny was getting a drug through a standard gravity-fed drip, which he noticed was rather difficult for the busy nursing staff to control and monitor. He thought there must be an easier way. Initial research revealed that available drip monitors cost between $2,600 and $7,100 and so were reserved for the most critical patients.

Gallagher saw the potential for a low-cost drip monitor that could be attached to a standard gravity-fed drip. Drawing on his background as a control engineer, he developed a prototype device using a red light optical fiber system sensor. The sensor can count the drip rate and delivers an audible warning if the drip stops. One of these units costs about $700 — about a quarter of the cost of those previously available.

Despite no manufacturing or marketing experience, Gallagher decided to manufacture the product himself. With the help of a

Cardiff-based product design consultancy, he refined both the aesthetic and functional aspects of the prototype to create a "proper product" — which has since been developed even further. Newer models not only monitor the drip rate, but also incorporate data logging technology that allow essential information about the medication to be downloaded onto the device and used by hospital staff for better management of patient care.

## Clustering of firms

We commonly observe that similar firms tend to cluster together. Pittsburgh was once famous as the center of the steel and railroad equipment industries, Detroit for more than one hundred automotive firms, and Dayton for the beginnings of the aviation and auto parts industries, with nearly a thousand active innovators.

Today, semiconductor firms tend to be located around San Francisco in the area dubbed "Silicon Valley," while in their heyday mini-computer firms were almost all located in the Boston area. Roughly two-thirds of the world's thousands of new biotechnology firms are located in the United States, but the bulk of these are found in Northern California and New England. Milan is famous for fashionable consumer goods, while Sweden is much admired for its industrial equipment and products with ease and comfort of use, safety and health or ergonomic value.

Why have Boston, Silicon Valley, London, Stockholm, Milan and other notable locales spawned clusters of firms in one industry after another ranging from textiles, shipbuilding, shoe manufacture and machine tools to instruments, electronics, computers, software and biotechnology — over spans of more than a century? "Are there additional advantages inherent in integrated urban complexes that include universities and other research institutions, a large pool of skilled labor, easy movement of people from universities to firms and from firm to firm, availability of grants and venture capital, the presence of many lead users emphasizing product features and functions (often including the military and other government agencies), and the availability of design tools and services and a broad scope of other complementary products?"[36]

Clustering of firms defies standard economic explanations, which predict that producers and suppliers would be more widely distributed, all else being equal. The simplest and most direct explanation would be that co-location results from some resource advantage. Clearly, the wine industry is concentrated in areas that produce fine growing conditions for grapes.[37] An alternative explanation might be that firms collect near customers or in ways that make the search for a purchase more efficient. Thus, we see expensive retailers on Fifth Avenue in New York, while discounters are concentrated around Fourteenth Street.[38]

Seductive as these explanations are, and as obviously true as they are in limited cases, they seem to break down in general. Clustering of firms also defies the idea that today the much freer movement of goods and almost costless distribution of information and digital content makes firms free to locate almost without constraint. What might be the underlying processes that help us to understand what we actually see?

Perhaps what we see is the result of the concentration and ready availability of human capital and specialized skills. In this sense, people may not be as mobile or may be "stickier" resources than are goods or information. This explanation would certainly account for the presence of large universities concentrated on science and technology in places such as Boston, San Francisco, and Stockholm and on design in Milan. A large number of skilled individuals co-located with a large number of specialized firms provide a rich and flexible range of employment possibilities.

All things being equal, clustering seems to be enhanced by urbanization and reinforced by economic growth. Clustered suppliers seem to lead to greater efficiency. Larger and more diverse clusters seem to provide more scope for the combination of resources, brokering of ideas, and the collision and synthesis of different currents of invention.[39] Finally, it seems that larger and more diverse clusters are more resistant to economic shocks than are smaller or more narrowly focused ones.[40]

Another possible explanation is the existence of a nucleating parent firm. For instance, more than half of the electronics firms in Silicon Valley, including Intel, can trace their origins at least in part to a single enterprise. That nucleating firm, Fairchild Semiconductor, itself fissioned from the earlier Shockley Semiconductor, which was set up by William Shockley.[41] Digital Equipment seems to have played a similar role in the Boston area, and perhaps Microsoft is doing so today within the complex of software firms around Seattle.[42] One might guess that the more rapidly growing a nucleating firm is and the greater the market potential of its chosen technology, the greater will be its creation of so called spin-off firms. This is due to the fact that a single firm may simply not be able to pursue and take advantage of all the opportunities that arise in such a rich environment. Still, the presence of a strong nucleating firm seems more the exception than the rule.[43]

Conceding all of the above arguments, the observed phenomenon seems to be much more pronounced in the authors' view than can be accounted for by these explanations. If so, something deeper must be at work. A possible answer lies in the idea that information seems to be almost as reluctant to flow as are people, and this may be because information moves most effectively when it is carried in person. It is easy to assume that information is always clear and codified.[44] While this may be approximately true for some of the sciences, it is much less so for engineering and technology, and even less so for design and aesthetics. Indeed, most knowledge in these fields seems to be tacit, embedded in experiences and subject to interpretation. Thus, to communicate requires conversation, negotiation, modeling, drawing, demonstration, experiment, and explanation. Tacit information is, by definition, difficult to write down or index with precision. Hence, it is also difficult to possess exclusively, to appropriate, or to patent tacit knowledge. In a sense, it is within the state of the art. It is also clear that people tend to search for all information, and especially tacit information, first in their local neighborhood and among their closest and most trusted sources, reaching out further in general only when these do not suffice.

Thus, we believe that the importance for the creative process of firms' proximity to one another is greatest when the information they require is tacit or rapidly changing.

These arguments suggest that we should expect more spin-offs and more rapidly growing clusters when greater technological opportunity is coupled with low appropriability. The greater the number and the lower the cost of communication channels, the greater will be the number of ideas and innovations that tend to be created.[45] Knowledge usually flows from the science base into practice when individuals leave universities and laboratories for employment in industry. We speculate that a more rapidly growing industry would attract more young employees or entrepreneurs, and therefore a more rapid diffusion of knowledge and enhancement of technological opportunities from the science base. These are ideal conditions, in other words, in which to find design firms, venture capital firms, patent attorneys, and other innovation services.

With respect to the United Kingdom, design firms show a strong concentration in and around London. London alone accounts for more than half the fees and volume of work of British design firms. By comparison, London accounts for only about 16 percent of Great Britain's economy. Exhibit 3.6 illustrates just such a regional cluster. Why this London cluster, especially when there appears to be an increasingly functional separation and spatial separation between production activities (based in the north and overseas) and the creative service-based economy

## Why Clusters?

Our central argument about clusters is this: "[T]he location of innovative businesses is primarily a function of personal communication networks and contacts. The authors have been host to many visiting delegations of dignitaries and scholars each seeking the secrets of the complexes of entrepreneurial firms located around Boston on Route 128 and by implication around San Francisco Bay in Silicon Valley. One is often reminded of the parable of the blind men and the elephant. Bankers seek the keys to success in studies of venture capital and finance, professors in flows of research funds to local universities, developers in real estate markets and science or technology parks, politicians in government programs and so forth. While all of these are undeniably helpful and taken together valuable, we think that the primary factors of importance lie in the skills and knowledge of people in a region, in the capabilities and flexibility of corporations, and in the sophistication of and encouragement by their customers."[46]

concentrated in London and Southeast England? The clustering we see among British design firms seems to stem from the tacit nature of design work, which compels designers to remain close to each other so that they can communicate information that is not easily transmitted over distances. Clearly, the need for more frequent and *informal* communication is greater for design activities than for production.

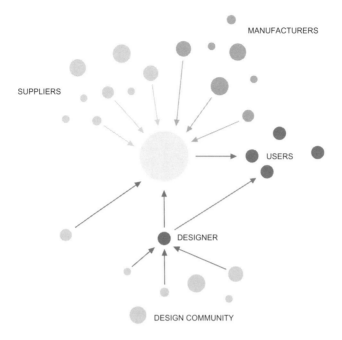

**Exhibit 3.6.** A regional cluster of design consultancies, suppliers, and manufacturers.

Clustering figures prominently throughout this book. We will see examples of design firms clustering in the Boston area, Sweden, and Milan, and we will return to this concept in several specific product cases, where the link between design firms and other industries similarly clustered will be explored.

**Freeplay's Wind-up Products**

In 1993, Trevor Baylis heard the narrator of a TV program on AIDS in Africa say that if people could only hear how to avoid the disease, its spread could be dramatically slowed. Unfortunately, Africa's low literacy rate kept the written word from getting out, and little electricity and expensive batteries made broadcast media a difficult option. Trevor had what he later described as a "Eureka moment." He recalled:

> "I stepped through to my workshop, with the narrator still talking in the background, picked up a battery transistor radio and soldered the battery connections to an old DC electric motor, which I knew worked as a dynamo when run in reverse. I then jammed the motor in the chuck of a hand drill where the drill bits are usually held, gripped the handle in a vice grip, and turned the drill's wheel. The dynamo turned, generated electricity, and the transistor burst into life. This all happened before the final credits rolled."[47]

Like Dyson with his bagless vacuum cleaner, Baylis experienced rejection after rejection when he sought to put his idea into production. "I must have gone to hundreds of companies, and almost all of them treated me like I was an idiot."

Eventually, though, a new company called Freeplay Europe took up and developed his ideas. In addition to the wind-up radio, Freeplay has also developed lanterns and torch lights powered by wind-up cranks and lights and radios charged by solar power or wind-up/solar combinations. The company pays considerable attention to users and the environment within which products will be used.

One Freeplay product, the self-powered Lifeline radio, is designed specifically for children, distance learning, and humanitarian projects.

The radio is rugged, colorful, easy-to-use, and receives excellent AM, FM, and SW reception. Its features include an easy-to-replace antenna made of an ordinary piece of wire, a rainbow-shaped dial scale with large print for easy reading, and a winding handle on the back — easily gripped by a child — that can be turned in either direction to charge the radio. Fully charged, the Lifeline can play for up to 24 hours. It also includes a solar panel housed in a detachable waterproof casing.

Freeplay's goal is "to provide freedom and independence through reliability. The result of achieving this goal is empowerment." The company is committed to balancing the imperatives of both profit and social justice — providing returns to shareholders whilst maintaining complete integrity and contributing to the personal fulfilment of its employees, the communities in which it operates, and the users of its products.

**Endnotes**

---

[1] "Nike, Apple to develop iPod running gear: system would allow shoes and player to teach performance," *Boston Globe*, 24 May 2006, p. E2.

[2] See J.M. Utterback, 1994, especially Chapter 9, for a detailed discussion of these points.

[3] V. Walsh, 1996.

[4] This is especially the case in what B. Verspagen and C. Werker (2003) call "the invisible college of the economics of innovation and technological change."

[5] The over-concentration on so-called high-tech, R&D-intensive activities is not new, and was one of the principle motivators for the development of the OECD's "Oslo Manual" and the European Community Innovation surveys that have followed (see OECD, 1992).

[6] Walsh, 1996.

[7]P. Gorb and A. Dumas, 1987.

[8]Walsh, 1996.

[9]Walsh, 1996.

[10]In the upper left quadrant, design is essentially concerned with symbols and communication — such as through graphics and branding. This is not the focus of interest for this discussion.

[11]T. Maldonado, 1964.

[12]V. Walsh *et al.*, 1999.

[13]N. Cross, 1995.

[14]S. Moody, 1980.

[15]Moody, 1980. Also, in discussing "function follows form," there is — as shared by the President and CEO of Design Continuum Gianfranco Zaccai — a third category which is "function following meaning," since "form" suggests a styling focus of the design process, while the better designers concentrate on uncovering human values and translating that into a more holistic experience with a product and service, or what has been referred to as "gestalt" — best exemplified in the Apple story.

[16]V. Walsh, R. Roy, M. Bruce, and S. Potter, 1992.

[17]Design Council, 1992.

[18]Moody, 1980.

[19]S. Pugh, 1991.

[20]C. Freeman, 1992. Quoted in Walsh *et al.*, 1992.

[21]B. Archer, 1976. Quoted in Walsh *et al.*, 1992.

[22]Walsh *et al.*, 1992.

[23]Walsh *et al.*, 1992; M. Akrich, 1995.

[24]R. Rothwell, 1986.

[25]J.M. Utterback and W.J. Abernathy, 1975; W.J. Abernathy and J.M. Utterback, 1978; P. Anderson and M.L. Tushman, 1990.

[26]For a full discussion, see Abernathy and Utterback, 1978.

[27]T. Pinch and W. Bijker, 1987.

[28]Presentation by James Dyson at MIT, 26 April 2006.

[29]In 1992–1993, the Hoover vacuum cleaner company offered to free return airline flights to customers who spent more than £100 on one of its products. Thousands of customers who qualified were never able to get their flights, and eventually lawsuits were launched. The ensuing settlements and bad publicity cost Hoover some £48 million and the episode has come to be known as one of the premier disasters in business public relations.

[30]By comparison, in 2002 British industry spent about £2 bn on external R&D, and there were around 1,000 R&D enterprises with some 9,000 employees.

[31]B. McAlhone, 1987; A. Sentance and J. Clarke, 1997.

[32]Meanwhile, J. Howells notes that in real-terms expenditure on external R&D doubled in the United Kingdom between 1985 and 1995, while total business

expenditure on R&D (BERD) grew by just 14 percent. Consequently, external R&D as a proportion of BERD nearly doubled, from 5.5 to 10 percent (Howells, 1999).

[33]One might ask what keeps the design firms from doing it on their own. The arrangements described here raise issues of power and dependency (see R. Coombs *et al.*, 2003), and while the designer and manufacturer will become interdependent, the extent to which their interdependence is symmetric is open to question.

[34]Note that the firms may not be undertaking only one activity, or even only one design activity. For instance, some of these firms may be manufacturers that also provide design services for other firms, but the size recorded is the firm's total employment. Moreover, some firms that engage only in "design activities" are, in fact, engaged in a variety of design activities. For instance, 133 firms are recorded as being engaged in both product and engineering design.

[35]They may be seen as "articulators" of tacit knowledge, where articulation is a process of expression through drawings, plans, models, and so on.

[36]J.M. Utterback and A.N. Afuah, 1998.

[37]L. Canina, C.A. Enz, and J.S. Harrison, 2005.

[38]G. Ellison and E.L. Glaeser, 1999.

[39]As suggested by B. Harrison, M.R. Kelley, and J. Gant, 1996.

[40]E.J. Malecki, 1985.

[41]P. Almeida and B. Kogut, 1999.

[42]R. Pouder and C.H. St. John, 1996, p. 1176.

[43]A.K. Klevorik, R.C. Levin, R.R. Nelson, and S.G. Winter, 1995.

[44]Almeida and Kogut, 1999, p. 908.

[45]Klevorik, Levin, Nelson, and Winter, 1995, p. 186.

[46]Utterback and Afuah, 1998, p. 184.

[47]N. Skeens and E. Farrelly, 2000.

# Chapter 4

## *MANAGING THE DESIGN PROCESS*

We have seen that simply producing a product that functions well is not enough to ensure success in the market. Something more is required, and we have expressed that something as "elegance," "customer delight," and "simplicity." By thoroughly examining the sales and product lives of an entire genre of competing products we discovered that only a tiny fraction can be judged truly successful. These exemplars exhibit much longer product lives as well as greater sales, and capture the lion's share of the market and profits.

The one or two firms that create the "classic" designs seem to have done so not by producing a plethora of variations and rushing them to market as many voices advise. Rather, they have carefully devised the architecture and user interfaces of their products, always keeping the users' experiences and values in mind. A classic product may often be based on technologies and components identical to those used by its designer's competitors, but through the design concept and design integration the product is given vastly greater salience and meaning in the eyes of the customer.

We have also seen provocative evidence from surveys conducted in the United States and the United Kingdom that firms are depending — to an ever greater extent — on designers, engineers and others outside their traditional boundaries for a large part of their vital and strategic innovation and product development. Further, firms are relying on suppliers as sources of technology and components. This trend might well be thought of as evolving toward greater degrees of so-called "open-source" innovation in an increasing number of products, services, and markets; indeed, there is tantalizing evidence that leads to this conclusion.[1] These circumstances demand that to succeed one must create a superior product or service idea, and must be prepared to invest in whatever effort is required to "stay in this business forever."[2] Alternatively, one might reach defensively for such empty strategies as "scale" or "critical mass" or engage in a whirl of usually fruitless and disappointing acquisitions.[3]

We contend that the only way to escape the winds of "creative destruction" is to provide superior products and services consistently to customers and to increase the degree to which products and services are integrated. This is a hugely demanding goal and one that even superior firms often fail to meet. That Sony, which outdistanced the competition with its personal music players, failed when confronted with digital music in the form of the Apple iPod is not the exception, but the norm. Three of four firms that lead in one product generation seem to fail to lead in the next, despite that they routinely pioneer new technologies — as Sony did in digital technology. Something more is required. The vulnerability of established firms is acute when the new product concepts stimulate rapid market broadening and expansion, as have digital media of all forms.[4]

In this chapter we begin a series of investigations into the *how* of design-inspired innovation. How might ideal designs — design *classics* — be conceived and created? Given many possible concepts, combinations, and prototypes, how might synthesis and integration of ideas be successfully achieved? What tools are necessary for the experiment and variation involved? What are the existing and emerging tools for synthesis?

With these questions in mind, the authors visited leaders of design firms in Boston, Sweden, Lombardy, and in the extended community of designers focused on mobility, wheelchairs, and wheelchair sports. This and subsequent chapters present the ideas and answers from our investigations.

**An ideal design**

A design may be thought of as being defined by its subsystems and by their interfaces or connections. Subsystems in turn may be collections of components having their own defined interfaces or simply single components. Focus on the ensemble of subsystems — that is, on the synthesis and integration of the whole — is what in our mind constitutes the process of design. Pursuing the improvement or ultimate performance of one or a few components at a time may be important in the course of progress, but rarely results in a timeless product design or design classic. Conversely, a new and original synthesis may not incorporate new technology, but it may provide for a whole new regime of performance and progress. In the world of engineering, this is also referred to as defining a product architecture in the abstract, or perhaps a product platform when referring to a specific product and its variants or models.

One need not search far from the most immediate needs for energy conservation to find examples. Combined electric generation systems are the synthesis of a gas turbine generator and a steam turbine generator to take advantage of the high outlet temperature of the former to generate steam for the latter. This seemingly simple idea has more than doubled the efficiencies of the two units used separately. Another example of design synthesis is provided by the hybrid car. A hybrid combines a standard internal combustion engine and generator with equally well-tested batteries and electric motors to improve the joint efficiencies of both. When the car does not need the entire power of the engine, the surplus is used to charge the batteries. When a surge of energy is required, both the engine and generator and the batteries join in to turn the electric motors. The overall efficiency of the whole is substantially improved.

A critical problem in the synthesis of designs and products is that of sub-optimization — that is, the problem of losing track of the whole by focusing too assiduously on the parts. A law in this field holds that when each part is optimized it is impossible for the design as a whole to be ideal. For the design as a whole to be ideal, compromises must be made in the selection or design of components to allow them to connect and work together. To illustrate the point, Iansiti mentions downhill skier Franz Klammer, who triumphed in every World Cup race for a season without winning a single partial event. He did so by posting the best *overall* combination of times in the "system" of races.[7]

### The Power of Synthesis in Design

The Douglas DC-3 aircraft offers a dramatic example of the potency of synthesis of disparate elements. The DC-3 was actually the first modern airplane and one of the most successful product designs of all time.

While perhaps not familiar to readers who have grown up in the jet age, this aircraft was a culmination of previous innovations and set the standard for commercial aircraft for two decades. Never the largest, fastest, or longest-range aircraft, it was nevertheless large enough and fast enough, and was the most economical plane capable of flying long distances. This aircraft satisfied market needs so well, in fact, that no major innovations were introduced into commercial aircraft design from 1936 until jet-powered aircraft appeared in the 1950s.[5]

This remarkable aircraft, which ruled the skies for nearly 30 years, was based on few original innovations. Rather, it was a brilliant synthesis of 33 ideas, each of which had been tested singly or with one or two of the others in earlier aircraft. These ideas included many now taken for granted: retractable landing gear, shrouded engines, all metal construction, and slotted wings.[6]

Ackoff illustrates this point with the example of designing a car. Suppose, he suggests, that we lined up all of the cars currently in production and then selected the best of each sort of part, fuel injectors, pistons, and so on from the set. We would have a complete set of the best-designed and best-performing parts, but with no possibility of assembling them to construct a functioning car. In fact, it would probably be impossible even to put them together. The only feasible way to design a working car is to start from a concept of the whole, or at minimum of its major functioning sub-systems, and then proceed to design or select appropriate parts. The essence of design is *wholeness* and *integration*. Understanding each component and making the best component is not a winning strategy, but it is often the implicit path that we take.[8]

A compelling example of the power of synthesis in design, as we will see in the section below, is provided by Alvin Lehnerd from his design work at the Black & Decker Company. Starting with a set of consumer power tools that had been designed and expanded over a number of years, Lehnerd decided to redesign the company's entire product offering at once. Each product had been designed to be best for its time and market circumstances, but that did not make Black & Decker's offerings as a whole appropriate for the future, another sort of sub-optimization. Lehnerd and his group began with a "clean sheet of paper" to determine what set of offerings — designed together — would work best as an integrated whole.

Both Lehnerd and Ackoff speak of making an "ideal design." In other words, if the product or product line could be anything we wanted it to be *here and now*, what would it be? Both then suggest that we should imagine ourselves as being the product or imagine being in those circumstances as if they currently existed. Standing in that place in our imagination, is there a set of feasible steps back to current resources and knowledge that would allow us to create a feasible migration path working back to our starting point in the other direction? If not, might we slightly modify the goal to create a feasible path?

We are typically taught to define a goal (or, formally, a criterion function) and then to list constraints of resources, time, distance, and so on. The primary optimization problem we deal with every day is to ask how much of our goal we can achieve given the constraints to which we are subject. We often frame this by asking three questions: Where are we today? Where would we like to be? What is the next logical step to take toward our goal?

Ackoff claims that such an approach will normally achieve at best about one-fifth of our personal potential, or of a design's true potential. In analytical terms, he is asking us to focus on the *dual* or mirror image of the optimization problem. To do so, we must begin by ignoring constraints and asking what would we like to be doing or what should our ideal design be if it could be anything we wanted. The answer must meet two tests. If we were that person and in that ideal place, or if we had that ideal design in hand, it must be possible for us, or it, to exist in the world as it is. In other words, we still cannot have perpetual motion or break the laws of thermodynamics. And the goal must be legal and ethical. Having set the goal, we must now ask which constraints we must relax or change and by how much to meet that goal or create that wonderful design. Not accepting the constraints as given creates an entirely different approach, one that is less readily conceived. That may well be the essence of a design process.

One can seldom relax all of the constraints necessary to achieve a stated ideal. When this happens, Ackoff urges us to step a short distance away from our ideal design to see whether something close to it can be achieved. In this manner, we are much more likely to set and to achieve an ambitious goal. Experience suggests that working to relax constraints, rather than optimizing within constraints, results in our reaching about four-fifths of our greatest potential in any pursuit including design.

As an example, let us further examine the Black & Decker case. In Lehnerd's terms, an ideal or conceptual design will examine the connections between each member of a product family. What elements do all members of the family share in common? Analysis of the Black & Decker power tool family showed that the key element was the electric motor, followed by housings, gearing, switches, and so on. A major project was launched to design a modular motor, coil, and armature with plug-in connections. The design was highly suited to automatic manufacturing and motor balancing and, by employing a hexagonal shape, greatly reduced materials waste. The resulting motor could be extended to serve in tools requiring from 60 to 750 watts of power with no changes in materials, manufacturing, or connections between components.[9] The same motor design is now in use worldwide for a range of voltages and frequencies of current.

At the beginning of the project, Black & Decker produced thirty different motors, 60 motor housings, and 140 armatures, each requiring its own set of machining tools. With such variety, the company was required to keep thousands of types of parts in inventory, which increased the cost and complexity of manufacture and multiplied possible sources of error. By redesigning its entire product line at once and simultaneously streamlining manufacture, Black & Decker was able to reduce labor costs by 85 percent and reduce materials cost by 40 to 85 percent. Similar simplification of other sub-systems such as gears, motor housings, switches, and cord sets was carried out as well, resulting in a massive reduction in variety and cost of all parts used by the company. As a result, the customer experiences benefits such as cost savings and increased reliability among a wider range of available products.

Let us look in more detail at some of the specific aspects of product design.

**Architecture and modularity**

The first aspects we will explore are *architecture and modularity*. We defined product architecture above as a map in the abstract of sub-systems and their interfaces or connections. One might think of a product design as a specific instance of a given architecture. Thus, the Sony Walkman products all share the same basic architecture of reading head, tape drive, controls, and ear-phones. The many variations of this architecture can therefore be created and produced relatively inexpensively to address different tastes and price levels in the market. To achieve this capability, Sony worked first for a number of years to perfect both the architecture and its basic elements and interfaces.

Black & Decker's modular motor and housing design also allowed rapid extension of their product family to new groups of tools such as rotary shears. At the height of its project, the company was launching a new tool model every three weeks, and was able to develop completely new tools using combinations of well-tested modules in less than six months. As a consequence of the rising quality and variety of its tools combined with dramatically lower pricing, Black & Decker grew tenfold in a decade from annual sales of $200 million at the start of the project to more than $2 billion a decade later.[10]

A key point is that to achieve exceptional success the entire market must be considered and addressed in a dynamic manner. Constantly migrating toward the corner of the market that accepts higher prices and affords higher margins for products offering maximum performance should be seen as a dangerous trap. Such a high-end strategy opens the firm to competition from rivals that offer simpler and less expensive models. With the advance of technology, simpler products may quickly progress to offer performance acceptable to more demanding customers as well, and quickly invade the high-price, high-margin space. Today, one can buy a Toyota Lexus that is at least as good as the once unchallenged luxury cars, but for about half the price. A robust strategy for growth and competition virtually requires any competitor to address the entire market, as did Sony and Black & Decker in the examples above, and to be the lowest-cost producer of the basic version of the product. Design firms may well be more aware of the segments and price points that exist in the market than are their clients, as they integrate across a broad range of client commissions.

Exhibit 4.1 illustrates some of the many types of modularity that a designer can use to create a broad and varied range of models of a given product architecture. For example, Propeller Design's saddle illustrated in Chapter 1 employs a combination of component swapping and cut-to-fit modularity to fit each saddle to the measurements of a particular horse and rider and provide types for different competitive events. The Dyson case discussed in Chapter 3 and the Metamorfosi case to be described in Chapter 6 both employ the sharing of a central component to create a range of variety in vacuum cleaners and lighting, respectively.

Exhibit 4.1 illustrates some of the ways one might think of creating variation through modularity. A re-chargeable battery shared among

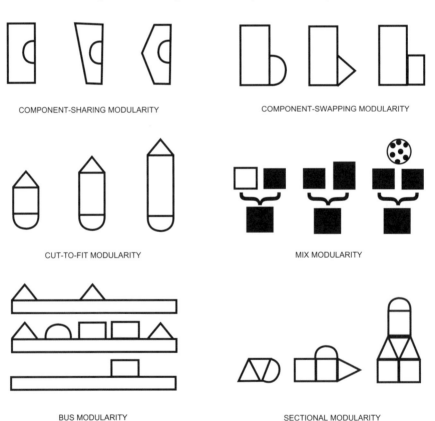

Exhibit 4.1. Various modes of modular design.[11]

various tools such as a drill, jigsaw, and sander is an illustration of component sharing. Sharing the battery reduces expense but, more importantly, it allows one battery to be constantly charging or ready while the second is in use. Component swapping might be illustrated by the example of a drill that can also be used with a sanding disc or a grinding head. Cut-to-fit modularity is the classic case of tailored suits. Levis has extended this theme recently to mass-customized blue jeans. A range of sizes of each piece of a pair of jeans is kept in inventory. After a customer is measured, a computer program makes a selection of components, which are then sewn together into a pair of jeans "tailored just for you." Not only is a customer better satisfied, the retailer also obtains extra revenue from the service.

Mix modularity is experienced each time we walk into a paint store or a Chinese restaurant, where a wide variety of colors or meals can be compiled from a small stock of pigments or ingredients. Bus modularity is encountered in our daily use of a computer or a telephone system in which all the various components are coordinated by means of a standard communication path, which makes it simple to install added parts. Most pre-fabricated building systems exemplify sectional or snap-together modularity; a classic example is the LEGO® block described in Chapter 2.

The point is not, of course, that Exhibit 4.1 exhausts all the possibilities — there may be many more. Rather, it is to show that a huge array of combinations, variety, and experimentation can be achieved by taking a modular approach. More readily developed and more robust designs are the result.

Pavitt[12] finds that modular product architectures in which components and interfaces are standardized and interdependencies among components are de-coupled is of increasing importance in dealing with product and technological complexity. He notes that this further enables the contracting of design and production of components and sub-systems to suppliers. Pavitt highlights the growth of "modular production networks" defined by points in the value chain where information can be made formal and highly specific. However, he states that this trend may not extend to "a neatly specified system for the production of innovations, with product and system designers, their sub-contractors for components and sub-systems, and their manufacturers working together through arms length relations."[13] The reason for this is, of course, the need to convey much tacit knowledge, as Pavitt emphasizes.[14]

The key to success, in Pavitt's view, is the central task of integrating different technologies that are progressing at widely varying rates. Design challenges in the auto industry provide a vivid current example. In cars, mechanical components that change slowly, over decades, must work with electronics, sensors, and communications technologies that change much more rapidly. Systems integration and perhaps provision for module updating and replacement is crucial to success.

Pine states that a modular design is virtually a prerequisite for products to be produced inexpensively but singly to suit individual tastes.[15] In Japan, Matsushita offers bicycle buyers 11 million options, based on a modular system. Before Propeller's modular saddle, most horse riders would be forced to purchase a good enough compromise from a narrower range of standard saddles. Poor saddle fit also caused back problems in about 60 percent of horses with which they were used.

A few top competitive riders would be fortunate enough to be able to obtain custom saddles suited to themselves, their mount, and their chosen event, but doubtless at high cost and following a long wait. Now more riders can surely do so. We will see this idea illustrated further in the extended case below of a DVD rental kiosk developed by Eduardo Alvarez and IDEO.

Another interesting example that exhibits the power of modularity is the development of a broadened product line for DeWalt Tools by Altitude, a Boston-based design firm. Using DeWalt's standard recharge-able battery pack (component sharing) in a worksite radio and battery-charger combination, Altitude produced what has become a design classic.

**Thinking Beyond the Toolbox**

When DeWalt, a leading US power tool manufacturer, asked Altitude to conceive new product ideas for the professional worksite, the recommendation — a radio — was certainly unexpected. But after intensive work and hundreds of creative collisions, the design team thought of combining the DeWalt brand with entertainment. With an industrial sound generator featuring an integrated battery charger, rugged controls, and a protective roll-cage, the designers developed a new *category* of radio.

Altitude researchers conducted in-depth and extensive interviews in the construction industry to understand what workers in steel-toed boots valued in a radio and discovered that there were significant opportunity gaps between incumbent products and the consumer's needs. Contractors were destroying and replacing three to four portable radios a year in their harsh worksite conditions. DeWalt's radio needed to communicate visually that it was "worksite tough" but wouldn't monopolize scarce power outlets. Integrating a charger that fits all of DeWalt's battery packs helped build fanatical loyalty and spurred sales of other DeWalt products.

"The Worksite Radio/Charger was a defining product for our DeWalt brand and for the entire cordless category," explains Bob Welsh, the company's global director of industrial design. "It has since become an unmistakable icon in the construction industry." Sales exceeded expectations, boosting profitability, achieving high margins, and selling for years with minimal price erosion. In fact, the Worksite Radio/Charger remains the most successful product launch in DeWalt's history. It illustrates how targeting specific market niches can facilitate the discovery of customer needs.

**Transparent interfaces**

An early question raised in the research for this book was whether the movement of the innovation and design process toward networks of actors (as shown in Exhibit 1.3) would open a producer of products and services to wider competition and predation. In fact, it is inevitable. Resistance will simply slow the pace of change for the firm trying to maintain a proprietary design and raise its costs, painting the firm into a corner. By the same token, customers will prefer to buy products that do not necessarily lock them in to a single vendor or set of services or software.

For modular design to deliver its maximum benefit, the interfaces between modules must be transparent and open rather than closed and proprietary. Transparent interfaces create a mixed blessing by opening up the supply chain for modules to greater competition. This makes the producing firm more vulnerable to outside influences and predators, but at the same time gives it and its customers a wider range of choices and increases the rate at which technology can advance and the breadth of its potential application. Notable examples in which a firm offering a superior but closed design have lost in a competitive race to firms with inferior but open designs include Sony's Betamax versus VHS video recorders, Apple's Macintosh versus the IBM personal computer, and Boeing's early suspended engine pod design, which allowed many jet engine choices, versus competitors' engines integrated in wing designs. In each case, the design that allowed more competition, and also more implicit partners, won the larger share of sales.

**Open standards and open source innovation**

Von Hippel contends that the locus of innovation is shifting toward user communities over time, and that if this is true it is a matter of great interest and relevance for the future. "Innovation communities," he writes, "can increase the speed and effectiveness with which users and also manufacturers can develop and test and diffuse their innovations. They also can greatly increase the ease with which innovators can build larger systems from inter-linkable modules created by community participants."[16]

"Open source software development is perhaps the most prominent example of the community-based model. Although often viewed as an anomaly unique to software production, the community-based model extends well beyond the domain of software. Innovative communities have been influential in product categories as diverse as automobiles, sports equipment, and personal computers." — Sonali K. Shah[17]

We know that design contests have been around for quite a while, but what is truly new is the global scale on which companies can now reach out to the best and brightest. For example, LEGO allows programmers from outside the company to access the code that controls its Mindstorm toy robot, leading to an increased range of activities the robot can perform, in ways the company never imagined.[18] Core 77, the industrial design site, teamed up with watchmaker Timex for a global design competition called Timex 2154: The Future of Time (celebrating Timex's 150th anniversary). Designers from more than 70 countries explored and visualized personal and portable timekeeping 150 years into the future, resulting in more than 640 entries. Winners can still be viewed online, and in the Timex Museum.

In the same vein, Illy Cafe teamed up with *Domus* magazine in April 2004, asking students and designers under the age of 35 to create new ways of enjoying coffee ("create a place for meeting, discovery and encounter"). Over a ten-month period, 704 entries were received, roughly half coming from outside Italy. The best fourteen projects were exhibited in Milan. The winning concept is an escalator that functions both as a coffee machine and an art show. Coffee is served at the bottom of an escalator. On the way up, customers sip their coffee and enjoy a brief art exhibition. At the top of the escalator, they throw their plastic cup into a recycling machine that instantly molds it into a ticket for an art exhibition or show.

In South Korea, mobile carrier KTF has held a contest to design new cell phones based on a "Cell Phone of Sensibility" theme, with a focus on usability and style. In late 2005, 19 winners were announced, and a few of them may see their creations end up in Korean stores relatively quickly. Another approach involving outside experts can be found at Procter & Gamble, which launched its dedicated Connect + Develop program (mentioned in Chapter 1) with the goal of having at least half of its new products derived from ideas generated by non-employee experts.[19] Beside its own research and development employee base of 7,000, the company now has access to millions of potential innovators. The results so far are everything from Swiffer Wet Jet, Olay Daily Facials, Crest Whitestrips, and Night Effects to Mr. Clean Autodry, Kandoo baby wipes, and Lipfinity.

In some respects, one might view the process of networked design and brokering that we describe as part of a broader movement toward more widespread participation in the creative process in all its aspects!

## The design and innovation system in Boston

We said in earlier chapters that there is a growing trend toward networks of firms participating in the innovation process, and that a growing number of these are design firms. Our survey in the United Kingdom showed evidence of an astonishing concentration of designers in and around London. Design and innovation are markedly an urban phenomenon. Recent evidence from others' research shows that, all things being equal, clustered suppliers seem to lead to greater efficiency. Larger and more diverse clusters of firms seem to provide more scope for the combination of resources, brokering of ideas, and the collision and synthesis of different currents of invention. Thus, we believe that the importance for the creative process of firms' proximity to one another is greatest when the information they require is tacit or rapidly changing.

These arguments indicate that we should expect more spinoffs and more rapidly growing clusters when greater technological opportunity is coupled with low appropriability. The greater the number and the lower the cost of communication channels, the greater will be the number of ideas and innovations that tend to be created. Hargadon and Sutton, from a case study of the design firm IDEO, suggest that design firms act as technology brokers by introducing solutions where they are not known and in the process create new products that are original combinations of existing knowledge from different industries.[20] They contend that designers exploit their access to a broad range of technological solutions with organizational routines for acquiring, storing, and retrieving this knowledge, and that organizations that face many different problems develop routines that will be broadly useful in solving future problems.

Boston has been a home for radical and innovative ideas from its very beginning. Founded by religious dissenters, Boston has been a source of revolutionary thought in realms as varied as governance, human rights (the abolition of slavery and universal suffrage), science, medicine, and the arts. During the past two centuries, the focus of this ferment and energy has expanded to innovation and manufacturing in various fields of design and technology. Rapidly growing clusters of new ventures in information technology, software, electronics, medical instruments, and biotechnology have supplanted earlier communities of firms in the realms of tools and machinery, furniture, textiles, defense, and scientific instruments. There are large and growing communities of firms in finance and financial services, design services, intellectual property law, and others that support this dynamic, as well as large universities and hospitals with major laboratories and research programs. In recent years, biotechnology has been a major focus of growth, especially in venture capital investment.[21] Today, more than 400 of the United States' approximately 2000 new firms in biotechnology are located around Boston, a disproportionate number (per capita) equaled only in California. This complex is shown schematically in Exhibit 4.2.

We show in the exhibit that there is an incredibly rich texture of communication links among all of the actors in the Boston innovation and design complex though this is possible only to suggest. We surmise that the more actors there are in a complex, the more diverse and varied

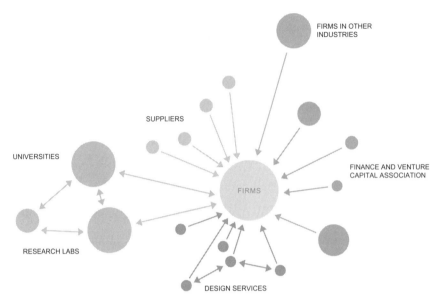

**Exhibit 4.2.** A schematic of actors in the Boston design and innovation cluster.

are these actors. Further, the richer the degree of communication links among them, the greater will be their propensity to innovate. This is certainly borne out by a comparative study made by Rickne of firms developing medical implant technologies and devices in Boston, Cleveland, and all of Sweden.[22] Areas with greater diversity and connectedness would enable and encourage many more creative collisions and combinations than would be the case in areas sparsely populated with technology-based firms or having firms that are sparsely connected. Based on this hypothesis, one would expect less innovation in Cleveland and in Sweden than in Boston; in fact, that is what the data suggest.

Hargadon and Sutton contend that when connections are made, existing ideas often appear to be new and creative as they change form, combining with other ideas to solve the problems of different users.[23]

Brokers, in their view, benefit from disparities in the level and value of particular knowledge held by different groups, and derive value by enabling the flow of resources between otherwise unconnected groups within a larger network. In their analysis, technology brokering is visible at the level of firms and industries, but it takes place through the actions of teams and people.

### Enabling Innovation Through Knowledge Brokering

To recognize the potential value of a technology and adapt it to disparate products, designers must be familiar enough with a technology to generate analogies appropriate for current designs. Links to many industries provide designers with access to a broader range of technological solutions than they would see working in a single industry.[24] A case study of Thomas Edison's early laboratory in Menlo Park suggested that he created a setting, and ways of thinking and working, that enabled his inventors to move easily in and out of separate pools of knowledge, to keep learning new ideas and to use ideas in novel situations.[25] Researchers suggest that there are four tactics to enabling innovation through knowledge brokering: explore new territories, learn something about everything, find hidden connections and make prototypes that work.[26]

As one might expect, the Boston area provided us with a great variety of design firms from which to select examples for our study. We interviewed leaders at Product Genesis, Bleck Design Group, Herbst Lazar Bell, Product Insight, Altitude, Design Continuum, Manta Product

Development, Synectics, IDEO, and 9th Wave, as well as at the MIT Media Laboratory and its associated AgeLab.[27] Each of the companies is a product development firm. In addition to offering industrial design services, these firms have a suite of additional services for their clients. Although varying from firm to firm, the expanded services include mechanical and electrical engineering and analysis, software programming, product and marketing strategy, rapid prototyping, and manufacturing. In the course of the work, one of our authors, Eduardo Alvarez, developed an idea for his own business and worked for an additional year with IDEO to develop the idea and several prototypes for test. He has since raised seed capital, started the company, and launched the product in one national market. This experience is described below as an extended case study of VIGIX.

## VIGIX Inc.

Our case begins with the objective of creating a truly fulfilling customer experience. The VIGIX idea is to create a network of small-footprint kiosks — in convenience stores, supermarkets, office buildings, airports, and elsewhere — from which movies and games are sold and rented on physical media (DVDs and memory cards) and through direct downloads. The product was developed in partnership with IDEO, among the world's most prestigious design firms.

For the entrepreneur and his new company, the pursuit of customer delight has been the focus of product development. Two principles — simplicity and excellence — guided the design team as it first identified the requisite and most valuable elements in the perception and customer experience when renting a movie and only then turned to creating the technology and operational procedures to achieve the product objectives.

The product features include convenience, ease of use, and reliability. Small kiosks make it possible for VIGIX to be in convenient and non-traditional locations. Each kiosk offers only the 40 new titles most people are looking for, and a simple graphic user interface allows the customer to watch a video clip of the movie and see the customer rating the movie earned in theaters.

To ensure product competitiveness, the team designed a very simple kiosk. Movies are returned by mail with the provided postage-paid envelope, eliminating the need for a complex robotic arm to take DVD returns and restock them in the machine — as in competing kiosks. Having the customer mail the DVD eliminates the need for a much larger, higher-cost kiosk that requires more maintenance. The VIGIX kiosk is less than half the size of its competition, can be installed by one person, and is easily moved (and thus deployed in the market). High reliability is assured because there are no moving parts. Using a unique patented technology, the kiosks are restocked by a simple cartridge swap that can be done by anyone, with no training. Cartridges are restocked centrally, where the company can enforce strict quality controls, but restocking the kiosks is done by outside companies such as UPS.

VIGIX also enhances the customer's delight with its system for ensuring that titles customers want are available at the kiosks. Availability of titles can be checked at a website that duplicates the screen the customer sees when choosing a DVD at the kiosk. Customers can locate the kiosk closest to them and reserve titles.

*The Design Process*

The VIGIX team employed brainstorming, storyboarding, focus groups, customer observation, surveys, market tests with several prototypes, and a deep analysis of current and future competition to define the most valuable elements in customer perception and experience when renting a movie. The designers began by storyboarding situations in which convenient movie rental would make a big difference in the customer experience. Exhibit 4.3 shows a weekend car trip of a family with young kids. The kids soon become impatient and begin to fight. When dad spots a gas station with the VIGIX logo, he stops and rents a movie for the minivan's DVD. The unpleasant situation in the car is transformed. Later, dad drops the movie, in its return envelope, in a mailbox.

Visualizing such scenarios helped the team understand several important factors. For example, the scenario could be true only if there were a pervasive network of kiosks. When the product developers approached the largest US convenience store chains, they learned that the kiosks would have to be very small and stand alone in aisles, not against already used walls, if they were to have any chance of being

**Exhibit 4.3.** Story board of the envisioned customer experience in the early stage of the design process.

put in these stores. The kiosk would have to look good from the front *and* the back.

The VIGIX example begins with an ideal design or concept as we have defined it above. In this case, the team has been perceptive in seeing that the customer is not only the final consumer, but also that the vendor in whose premises the rental kiosk must reside and be serviced matters. The designers have stressed simplicity and ease of use and service in every phase of the kiosk's operation from installation through the customer interface and replacement of stock. Simplicity seems especially important, as the kiosk's host — the vendor — will be on the front line of any complaints from users, which must be kept to a minimum.

That the kiosk has built-in ease of response to meet varying demographics and changing demand seems a vital advantage over competitors, as does the entrepreneur's acute use of competitive intelligence and consumer testing in specifying the design. The product team has combined

**Exhibit 4.4.** The Vigix kiosk.

hardware, software, and web-based services in much the same way as the successful Apple iPod formula. Further, the team has used various visualization techniques — in this case, a storyboard, alternative scenarios, sketches, and models — to enhance communication and produce an elegant integration of various concepts.

A fascinating aspect of the case is that it has led to a patented breakthrough in vending machine technology and operation, which should have much broader appeal and application than in this product alone. The VIGIX kiosk and services have been tested and at this writing have been launched in an attractive market.

The VIGIX example highlights two aspects of the design process — *visualization* and *modeling* — that we have found to be central in design inspired innovation. The VIGIX designers relied upon both visualization and modeling to develop the kiosk. In Chapter 8, we discuss these aspects in considerable detail.

**Synthesis and integration**

How can a designer understand what the customer really needs? Our research finds that strong contact with the ultimate customers is one of the most common practices of successful product design organizations. Every leader of a design firm we talked with is an information enthusiast. They promote awareness of the world through collaborative communication with universities, encouraging their employees to teach, attending conferences, hiring freelancers and consultants, attending trade shows, and so on. Even with these practices, however, defining customer needs is a hard problem to crack. The more innovative the idea, the harder it is to determine customer needs, because there may be little or no information or culture around the future product. In other words, the information needed is almost entirely latent and unspoken, or tacit in academic jargon.

The design of a product is an exercise in blending both tacit and explicit knowledge to solve a problem. As Ed Gilchrest from 9th Wave Design noted during our conversation, the real asset "is the knowledge in the designer's head."[28] In other words, the knowledge that is codified or explicitly represented by a product is not as valuable as everything else a designer knows. The designer knows about the "why" and "how" of solving the design problem as well as the final answer. When the next design problem is presented, the designer may be unable to apply the same answer, but may very well be able to apply expertly the methods and reasons learned to find a creative *new* answer. Roger Bohn suggests eight stages of knowledge, ranging from complete ignorance (stage one) to complete knowledge (stage eight). When the most important knowledge is in the workers' heads, knowledge is at stage two — it is expertise based.[29]

Tom Allen was one of the first to describe the striking differences in communication patterns among scientists in contrast to those among engineers.[30] Scientists communicate in a markedly more formal and codified manner than do engineers, relying primarily on journals. Engineers operate more in the world of tacit communication and trade-offs. Informal conversations, drawings, models, and prototypes are the less precise bread and butter of engineering work. It is not surprising that working closely together enhances both the quality of communication and the results of engineering work.

The design of the Douglas DC-3 aircraft, including producing the prototype, involved only fifty people working together in one building for less than a year. The result was so good that the prototype was sold as production model number one! One of the first five DC-3s produced was removed from commercial service after five decades of service and now resides in the Smithsonian Air and Space Museum as one of the great design classics of all time.

The tacit nature of product design knowledge is fundamentally why face-to-face communication has been especially important in ensuring knowledge "blending." As individuals work together, they are able to build a rapport that facilitates knowledge transfer. Because personal communication is an essential part of tacit knowledge transfer, co-location would seemingly be critical to knowledge transfer between designers.[31] Product development firms recognize that knowledge transfer takes place both ways during product design collaboration. Product Genesis said this transfer begins with the initial interaction between the client and the firm.[32] Communication during design collaboration is the fundamental means of transferring knowledge.

"It is hard to transfer the full complexity of a technology ... If the receptor knows very little, he can do very little even with the simple idea, because he cannot generate the mass of detail that is required to put it into execution. On the other hand, if he knows a great deal and is capable of generating the necessary details, then from just a few sentences or pieces of technology he will fill in all the rest. That is why it is hard to transfer technology to the Third World and very hard not to transfer it to Japan."[33] In simple terms, the more similar the knowledge that two people have within a product domain, the more easily additional knowledge can be transferred between them. Davenport and Prusak also observed that a major factor in effective knowledge transfer is a common language about the knowledge domain.[34]

In a case study that looked at how knowledge transfer could be facilitated between a contracting company and a supplier, Tunisini and Zanfei found that the first investment that had to be made was the skill-intensive and time-consuming process of developing a shared language.[35] Product Genesis reinforced this idea in our conversations by saying that the key to knowledge transfer was the language used. When the firm embarks on a new product development engagement with a client, Product Genesis ensures that all participants understand a glossary of project-specific terms.[36]

By changing how designers work, technology advancements have changed the knowledge intensity of their output. A computer model's representations with links to enterprise-wide databases and other design models mean it contains much more actionable knowledge about the product and the design than drawings once did. As a result, the ability to learn from models has increased. Product Insight noted that its designers learn a great deal about clients' products from the clients' computer models.[37] Most product development firms we interviewed described how the Internet and effective search engines have made design research simpler, faster, and more productive, widening their sources of design knowledge for possible inclusion in the product.[38]

Sometimes in a complex project such as the design of a new car, an abstract model is insufficient, even if it is a vivid three-dimensional computer rendition. What is called for is a full-scale physical model, even though that may be extraordinarily costly. One of the present authors and seven of his students were involved from beginning to end in the development of the Chrysler LH platform, a basis for many of the company's current models. The project was so vital to Chrysler at the time that the company went to the length of devoting an entire large separate building to the LH team. All of the needed design and engineering groups were arrayed around the perimeter of the building. The prototype of the new design was placed in the center of the building so that it became the center for communication and a persistent reminder of the status of all of the design work and its integration. In Carlile's terms, the prototype was a "boundary object," a physical representation that helps solidify problem definition and focus discussion and coordination between members and sub-groups of the entire team.[39] Noehren extended Carlile's work on product development teams by showing that there was a statistically significant correlation between the frequency of boundary object usage by a product development team and the success of the project. Noehren also noted that models provide a more effective product development team communication focus than drawings.[40] This will be discussed further in Chapter 8.

The LH prototype was built from both standard and sometimes one-of-a-kind parts. An engineer working on the prototype in the center of the building was immediately obvious to all around. Others who were curious or simply walking by could observe any and all changes to the prototype and the manner in which these might affect or interact with their own parts of the project. As a result, the LH platform was one of Chrysler's most effective designs and was completed in record time.

The effectiveness of a boundary object in communicating knowledge about a design is a consideration in the location of design work. The more explicit the specification and information needed, the more mobile the process can be. Technology has changed the ability of designers to communicate through computer models and virtual three-dimensional representations. With manual drafting and drawings, the knowledge of the design resided in the designers' and analysts' minds. The drawing was a mute device for communicating a fraction of the knowledge about the product. Communication and effective knowledge transfer are influenced by having a common language, co-location and trust building, the use of boundary objects, and design process technology.[41]

Another change pointed out by the product development firms is the ability to create rapid prototype models directly from the computer model of the product. Firms we interviewed recognize intuitively that the prototype is an effective means of communicating knowledge about the design — it is a better boundary object. When prototypes are combined with virtual simulations made possible through advanced software linked to the engineering model, extensive knowledge is available about the configuration, behavior, and functioning of a product.

The complexity of many of today's technology products requires that input from many different disciplines be integrated into a final solution. Product development teams provide a way to "fuse" different ideas from different people working on the same problem, which ultimately is a major source of knowledge.[42] Design knowledge is not just in the designer's head, but is also in the heads of all those who helped in the integration of the solution. The integration of many different types and sources of knowledge in the context of a specific design problem is a significant contributor to a product's knowledge intensity, which, in turn, influences the degree of collaboration required for its completion. As the knowledge intensity of the product increases, the amount of collaboration necessarily increases. Ultimately, collaboration, of which communication is a part, is the knowledge transfer instigator between the supplier and the customer corporation.

Evolving design and engineering software and hardware enable a large complex integrated system, such as a commercial aircraft, to be designed and analyzed in a virtual three-dimensional environment. Entire manufacturing processes and factory flows can be simulated directly from the design models. Embedded within the models are data linked back to knowledge-based engineering software used to conceive the design and links to master lofted surfaces that span many parts. With the latest application releases, critical dimensions and tolerances can be portrayed in space. Changing the shape or parameters of a design feature can be propagated quickly through the computer model to modify any related features.

According to von Hippel, "Today, user firms and even individual hobbyists have access to sophisticated programming tools for software and sophisticated CAD design tools for hardware and electronics.[43] These information-based tools can be run on a personal computer, and they are rapidly coming down in price. As a consequence, innovation by users will continue to grow even if the degree of heterogeneity of need and willingness to invest in obtaining a precisely right product remain constant."[44]

The integration of many different requirements and technologies into a single product can be the significant differentiator between a successful and a poor product. Iansiti points out in his study of technology integration in the computer industry that the integration choices made during design, and not the technologies selected, can determine success.[45] In one case, the overall system performance of two mainframe processors was compared along with their fundamental component technologies. One processor achieved significantly better performance despite 10 of its 12 fundamental technologies being worse, and the remaining two on a par with the other processor. Better integration decisions were made by the first firm to develop a faster processor with poorer technologies.[46] Iansiti later shows how technology integration is an enabler for an organization to "view the entire product and production systems as a coherent whole, balancing the potential of individual technologies with the requirements of the context of application."[47]

### Integration Influences Collaboration and Knowledge Transfer

Consider the design of a fairing to enclose the radar on an aircraft. Peter Grant offers this as a good example of how integration can influence the collaboration and knowledge transferred.[48] Designing this product requires the integration of knowledge about materials and processes, structural analysis, weight analysis, aerodynamic flow, electromagnetic behavior, manufacturing processes (including cost), joint and attachment configurations, maintenance procedures, and potential damage scenarios (such as bird or lightning strike). Most of this knowledge is codified in many different forms, but how and why to select the various types of knowledge and integrate it is the uncodified designers' job. When the fairing is complete and installed on an aircraft, its external simplicity belies the knowledge intensity resulting from this complex design integration. If the design of such a fairing is contracted, integration knowledge necessary for the design will be transferred through the interactions of the corporation and the supplier. Sufficient collaboration must occur for the firm's needs to be understood by the design supplier for design execution.

The fairing design example also points to the impact of modularity on knowledge transfer. If the company so desires, the fairing design could be contracted with an outer defined surface, a mating interface definition, a weight and cost limit, and impact and electromagnetic requirements. Less knowledge about the rest of the aircraft would then be transferred to the supplier. However, for the corporation to develop this information requires sufficient specific knowledge and systems integration skills.

In a review of the literature on networks of innovators, Powell and Grodal conclude that the difficulty of transfer is high and the certainty of results low for tacit knowledge, while the opposite is true when knowledge is highly codified and formal. This leads them to suggest that "there is a medium range of knowledge codification where the value of the innovative output exceeds the costs of knowledge transfer and recombination."[49]

Our interviews suggest that the middle range is exactly the space in which design firms are most active and most effective.

Increasingly, design firms are providing more than the finishing touches. In a few cases, they are providing the total contract provision of innovation from start to finish. Most work lies in between these two ends of the spectrum. We develop this much more fully in the following chapter, based on our interviews in Sweden.

### The MIT AgeLab

Work at the Massachusetts Institute of Technology AgeLab, created in 1999, is a good example of how designers are pushing the boundaries of product development to "invent new ideas and creatively translate technologies into practical solutions that improve people's health and enable them to 'do things' throughout the lifespan." The AgeLab's efforts also illustrates the integration of product and service, hardware and software, into technologies and innovative delivery that "can have a signficant impact on the quality of life for older adults, their families and caregivers."

The AgeLab works in transportation, housing, health, communications, work and retirement, services, and decision-making around aging and caregiving. One example involves older drivers and new in-vehicle technologies. Collaborating with US, German, Japanese, and Italian automakers, a research team at the AgeLab is conducting extensive research on the design integration of intelligent transportation systems and their promise to promote lifelong safe driving. This includes an exploration of cognitive workload and the adaptation of new technologies to the driving tasks of operators over 50 years of age.

In the area of wellness and "self-empowered health," AgeLab designers have developed an Electronic Pill Pet that uses play and emotion to remind older adults to take their medications. And a Smart Personal Advisor transforms shopping for food and consumer health products into an informed activity. The advisor, mounted on a grocery cart, uses the consumer's personal diet information to provide guidance at the point of decision.

These are only a few of the projects at AgeLab, where design-inspired innovation is seen as "the opportunity to invent the future of healthy, active living."

**Endnotes**

---

[1]E. von Hippel, 2005.
[2]A. Lehnerd, 1987.
[3]M. De Rond, 2003.
[4]J.M. Utterback, 1994, Chapter 9.
[5]A. Phillips, 1971. Cited in Utterback, 1994, Chapter 4.
[6]R.E. Miller and D. Sawers, 1970.
[7]M. Iansiti, 1997.
[8]Lecture by Russell Ackoff in James M. Utterback's class at MIT, Cambridge, Massachusetts, 25 April 1989. Based on R. Ackoff, 1981.
[9]For further details, see Lehnerd, 1987; see also M.H. Meyer and A.P. Lehnerd, 1997.
[10]For a more recent example involving heart monitoring devices, see M.H. Meyer, P. Tertzakian, and J.M. Utterback, 1997.
[11]K.T. Ulrich and S.D. Eppinger, 2004.
[12]K. Pavitt, 2005.
[13]Pavitt, 2005.
[14]Pavitt, 2005.
[15]B.J. Pine II, 1993.
[16]von Hippel, 2005.
[17]S.K. Shah, 2005.

[18]LEGO Mindstorms Robotics Invention System 2.0 Software.

[19]L. Huston and N. Sakkab, 2006.

[20]A.B. Hargadon and R.I. Sutton, 1997.

[21]Massachusetts Technology Collaborative, *Index of the Massachusetts Innovation Economy*, 2005.

[22]A. Rickne, 2000.

[23]Hargadon and Sutton, 1997.

[24]Hargadon and Sutton, 1997.

[25]Hargadon and Sutton, 2000.

[26]A.B. Hargadon, 1998.

[27]Transcripts and summaries of the interviews can be found in E. Alvarez, 2000.

[28]E. Gilchrest, Interview at 9th Wave. Southbury, MA: 4 March 2000.

[29]R.E. Bohn, 1994.

[30]T.J. Allen, 1977.

[31]T.H. Davenport and L. Prusak, 1998.

[32]B. Vogel, 2000.

[33]R. Gomory, 1983. Cited in D. Leonard, 1998.

[34]Davenport and Prusak, 1998, p. 98.

[35]A. Tunisini and A. Zanfei, 1998.

[36]B. Vogel, 2000.

[37]J. Rossman, Interview with Product Insight. Acton, MA: 8 March 2000.

[38]According to Gianfranco Zaccai, leading firms such as Continuum have, for years now, applied design research based on qualitative analysis of human behavior and perceptions in contextual settings; this means that the user/customer actually becomes part of the cluster. This is a key first step which informs meaningful brainstorming, envisioning, and storytelling. In essence, the designer/researcher becomes the medium through which the user/customer/stakeholder communitcates their expressed aspirations. Eventually, probing into different aspects of human behavior associated with different product categories, the "users" also inform the design community's tacit knowledge.

[39]P.R. Carlile, 2002.

[40]W.L. Noehren, 1999.

[41]Carlile, 2002.

[42]Davenport and Prusak, 1998, pp. 49–50.

[43]von Hippel, 2005.

[44]von Hippel, 2005.

[45]Iansiti, 1998.

[46]Iansiti, 1998, pp. 79–81.

[47]Iansiti, 1998, p. 119.

[48]P.L. Grant, 2000.

[49]W.W. Powell and S. Grodal, 2005, p. 76.

# Chapter 5

## *THE WORK OF DESIGNERS*

The structure of relationships between design firms as providers of services and the corporations that are their clients is in a constant state of change. Sweden offers an opportunity for exploring this phenomenon and to outline the *types* of work in which designers engage. We use what we find in Sweden to make some more universally applicable comments in later chapters.

Sweden is, in many respects, a microcosm of the global economy. It is a small economy compared to the powerhouses of the world — the United States, Germany, and Japan, for example — but one in which we find all the industries typically found in these larger countries. On some measures, its economy is the world's most dependent on international trade, and from a list of the world's 1000 largest corporations, it would have the largest number of such firms on a per capita basis. Sweden has a global automobile industry, as well as telecommunications, pharmaceutical, textile, and other sectors not found even in other Nordic countries. In this respect, the country is an ideal laboratory for examining how design firms work and how they interact with their industrial clients. Further, Sweden tends to be a bellwether for changes that eventually surface in other countries.

Industrial design in Sweden takes place in five different settings, much like in other countries. Some larger companies have their own in-house design departments. Independent consultants offer their services individually or in *ad hoc* collaborations with others. Larger design consultancies (the largest having some forty employees) also offer their services to firms. Even engineering consultancies have discovered that they need to offer industrial design to comprehensively serve their clients. Finally, there are engineers and others who engage in design activities for their employers — although they are generally concerned with little more than functionality.

The Swedish design industry is in a state of flux as the country, like many others, increasingly emphasizes design as a national endeavor. Industrial design firms in Sweden must sell the idea that design is good business. Larger firms are employing more versatile and demanding tools — a development facilitated by computers and software development.

Several strong points characterize industrial design in Sweden. One is that it takes the view of the end user. Industrial design adopts a holistic approach, and designers are increasingly choosing materials and production methods for their clients and even assisting in establishing supplier networks. Concerns about ergonomics figure prominently. Further, we find in Sweden a growing use of visualization, which is discussed in further detail later in this chapter. Visualization makes communication easier, ideas tangible more quickly, and, in the rough sketch stage, allows designers to concentrate on the most essential aspects of the idea — the design, the product, the system, or even the service.

Even major companies with their own design departments may, from time to time, engage independent design consultancies, whether to augment internal resources or to spur creativity by giving insiders an element of competition. In some instances, large manufacturing corporations will engage two design firms simultaneously, believing that it will generate "creative friction" and, ultimately, better designs.

Design firms in Sweden are generally working in one of three Swedish "clusters" (Exhibit 5.1). The first of these is the transportation industry system located mostly on Sweden's west coast, in the region that includes Göteborg. Saab is located there, as are Volvo Car (now owned by Ford) and Volvo's truck and aircraft engine manufacturing divisions. Four of six Swedish design firms located around Göteborg

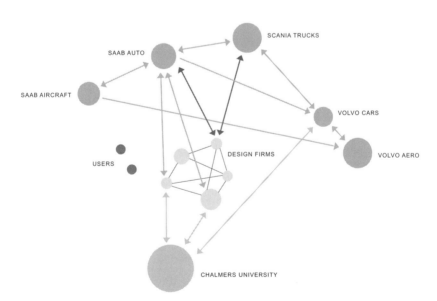

**Exhibit 5.1.** An example of a cluster of design firms in Sweden.

form a sub-system catering to transportation issues, although not exclusively, and offer services to their clients that range from providing finishing touches to internal designs, easing some of the design workload, to prototyping. GM's acquisition of Saab and Ford's of Volvo has meant an influx of design work to Sweden. Transportation equipment is developed with particular concerns for secrecy, life cycles, and legal and regulatory regimes.

Röhsska, Sweden's national design museum, is located in Göteborg, as is HDK, one of the country's leading centers for design education (School of Design and Crafts at Göteborg University). Industry and trade union representatives together recently recommended a partnership between unions and Göteborg universities (including the highly regarded Chalmers University of Technology) to create a unique research and education resource in the region focused on transportation.

The second grouping of interest is a design *output* cluster that has emerged with alumni from Sweden's oldest industrial design university, Konstfack, located in Stockholm (University College of Arts, Crafts and Design). These graduates have founded and staff many of Sweden's design consultancies. Demand, driven by the large part of Swedish industry located in the greater Stockholm area, has contributed to the growth of this design cluster.

The third system is broader in that it does not consist exclusively of "design" firms. So far, four large Swedish engineering firms have embraced the idea of integrating design into their services portfolio and have begun to establish strong design groups within the company — further evidence of the blurring of lines we discussed in Chapter 1. Within engineering firms, designers have comparatively easy access both to competencies and physical machine resources that a design consultancy might not have the ability to acquire on its own.

**Design firms' operations and processes**

Swedish industrial design firms are — or conceive themselves to be — either specialists or generalists. Some of the generalists refrain from *any* specializing, which they perceive as a danger (in the sense that "for the one who has a hammer, the whole world is a nail"). Firms that *do* see themselves as specialized often underline the importance of obtaining more varied experience and seek specific work outside their specialty. Some design firms include engineers or staff who are capable of taking on some engineering tasks; most of the firms claim to strive for diversity among the staff (diverse educational and cultural backgrounds). Still others augment their capability through regular but largely *ad hoc* collaborative arrangements. There are determined efforts to establish a presence internationally, through subsidiaries or just through the acquisition of clients abroad.

Many Swedish firms have been instrumental in bringing new knowledge from universities and institutes to influence product development projects with clients. Examples include a stringless guitar designed around new optical technologies. Another truly pushes the envelope of innovation: a conceptual design for an "artificial tongue" that would enable cooks sending and receiving recipes over the Internet to adapt their instructions and ingredients to local conditions so as to most closely replicate tastes across nations and cultures. Yet another design firm used its profits to create a research foundation to allow for more fundamental explorations beyond paid client work.

The firms profit from what they learn from individual clients and then leverage that knowledge and competency in their relationships with all their clients. Designers often bring together client firms from disparate industries.

Relationships between design firms and clients tend to be very long term. Projects that start small and limited often expand in scope as the client realizes that it makes sense to have the design firm continue further than initially envisaged. Large corporations tend to use a large number of design firms because they have numerous and differing needs.

More and more, design firms act as a product development department for the client, and all Swedish design firms can point to at least one or two projects or clients for whom they have been contracted to play a wider integration and coordination role. For some clients, this reflects the desire to contract as much as possible while limiting the number of suppliers. The designers themselves, however, may take the initiative and volunteer to coordinate additional functions. We see this most often in projects where the designers have come up with suggestions that are somehow outside the client's competency or frame of reference, such as suggesting new materials or production methods.

Designers in Sweden work in the same ways as do designers in other countries. While recommendations and awards may attract clients to certain designers, and many designers turn the companies for whom they did their graduation projects into long-term clients, competitions for design contracts have become increasingly popular. In competitions, ideas are the *main output*; the best ideas are rewarded by the design firm being selected for the contract. The client is rarely involved in generating ideas in the earliest stages of design. Alternatively, some designers work through an idea or concept generation process in which the client does initially participate. *Visualization* — another design approach — is where designers see themselves as excelling and contributing substantially to the clients' development, speeding it up and getting it right. *Mock-ups*, and later *prototypes*, are standard products of this stage. If a design firm does not feature a rapid prototyping machine internally, it will have a direct link to a company supplying that facility, remotely controlled by the designer. Depending on product type and the client's organization, the client sometimes produces detailed *drawings* and *production specifications*. Designers can also be engaged to design production tools for the products they are designing.

Design firms in Sweden use a number of different project-oriented techniques and tools for developing product concepts. There are several factors for success. One is to generate alternatives and variety. Another is to avoid becoming locked into one solution too early. Firms must steer clear or minimize preconceived or "tired" solutions. To achieve design-inspired innovation, they must go beyond the product objective itself to its wider presentation or promotion or function — ultimately delighting the end user.

There is certainly no one method of working. A majority of designers are convinced that sketching with pen and paper is both faster and more conducive to creative idea generation ("Computers aren't tactile," said one designer we interviewed). A small but equally vocal group contends that the computer is an even more versatile instrument that puts designers "closer" to the end product and allows them to sketch faster and more freely. Nor is there a monolithic view of whether to offer the client multiple options and suggestions. As one designer stated: "We know best, and the client has hired us to provide the very best, so one alternative will do." Others feel that it depends on the type of project. It is also a question of development stage: sketches may help a client better define the real issues, problems and needs.

Swedish design firms all claim to follow processes that are mostly standard and linear: some firms use specific tools and metrics. (In reality, processes are not always linear, but there is a feeling that clients wish to see understandable logic.) The leaders in ergonomic design often develop technical tools and measurement apparatus with highly innovative content to get the design "right." One firm relies on a design language of its own, which it is constantly refining and adapting. Another design firm established a knowledge bank covering a century's worth of developments in materials and their applications from which to draw ideas for a particular design project. Yet another firm distinguishes between different stages of brainstorming sessions, with and without clients' representatives.

Swedish designers frequently employ the brainstorming and value analysis techniques they learn in art school. They use analogies and metaphor to varying degrees. Playing the devil's advocate is more part of an individual's approach and style than a technique explicitly applied. Looking for a product's core function (e.g., "not a drill but a hole, not a hole but ...") is one avenue firms take.

Project teams at Swedish design firms are always temporary, and often include people from different backgrounds. Larger firms draw mostly on internal resources to achieve diversity, whereas smaller firms are more likely to network with outside individuals and organizations to assemble an "ideal" project team. Smaller firms may rely upon outsiders for focus group sessions, video anthropology, polling, and more. All Swedish design firms are involved, to one extent or another, in market studies (often employing specialized market research firms). The research is almost always tailored to give useful input to the design phase. It is market research data, rather than intuition, that most frequently result in designers advising a client not to go ahead with product development.

Since industrial designers are passionate about — almost indoctrinated in — representing the end user, most employ focus groups. The usefulness of focus groups depends upon the project. Video filming, interviewing, applying the practical instruments developed to gauge end-user behavior, simulations, and tests using electronic and other measurement tools all come into play at one point or another. Designers will often bring together specific groups of end users, engineers, behavioral scientists, artists, or even children because of their fresh views and knowledge of what is trendy.

Many Swedish designers swear to the importance of sketching. "Even failures in rendering a sketch as intended provide new food for thought and spur creativity," contends one very successful designer. Others sketch to translate ideas into tangible representations quickly. Sketches also serve as better communication tools than do words, eliminating many misunderstandings between designer and client. While a few firms see the computer as a substitute for a sketching board, all designers agree that visualization is at the core of the profession and is an important part of the design service. Among the clients of Swedish design firms interviewed, independent inventors in particular were impressed with the power of visualization; they often expressed awe at what the designer could make out of a crude idea the inventor is expressing for the first time. (Sketching is discussed in greater detail in Chapter 8.)

Information technology tools used by Swedish design firms include computer-aided design (there are a number of increasingly sophisticated CAD software products), but are not limited to CAD. Tool choice depends on the client and the project. For projects in the auto industry, for instance, specific tool requirements and new CAD software linked to computer-aided manufacturing have allowed the use of new forms and new styling elements never before possible. Sometimes designs must be delivered within a customer-stipulated software platform.

Rapid prototyping is a successor of CAD and allows the CAD program to control the machining to exact form. Since it is all made in one step and with one material, the result is most often a mock-up, not a functioning prototype. However, when the geometric (im)possibilities of intricate detail combinations that should fit together are tested and tried, the result may be more than a mock-up. The Internet and access to machines at a distance makes these resources available to smaller as well as larger design firms.

An important part of every Swedish design firm is its workshop of versatile and comprehensive machining tools. We should stress that despite rapid prototyping's allure, for the early stages many designers prefer hand tools to the versatile and comprehensive machines in their workshop. They make simple wooden or plastic mock-ups. If economically and technically feasible, a true prototype is always best, but often a replica in plastics or wood or sheet metal must suffice. If it functions at a basic level, it qualifies as a prototype. If it is just reproducing the product's physical form, it is a mock-up.

The same arguments of speed and costs associated with sketching are said to hold here as well. Some complicated and extremely costly systems may never be built as prototypes, but only conceived as final products.

While the designer always tries to take the end user's functional perspective, thus generating "wholeness," an engineer traditionally would prefer a company to organize products in families or on platforms for reasons of rationality, sharing tools, machinery, facilitating product development, handling and storing materials, and, of course, decreasing costs. The designer's point of view would be more about aesthetics, creating a uniform image where different products reinforce a commonality of purpose, quality, and the like. More and more, we see this perspective adopted by product engineers, thus affirming our view that the distinction between engineering and design is increasingly a relic.

**Design avenues to innovation**

Our discussions with design firms in Sweden reveal that there are a host of avenues to innovation involving designers (Exhibit 5.2). Clients and projects also vary greatly. A large internationally established company such as IDEO, which does not work in Sweden, is involved in a very different set of activities than is the Swedish firm Go Solid, whose three designers focus on assisting inventors.

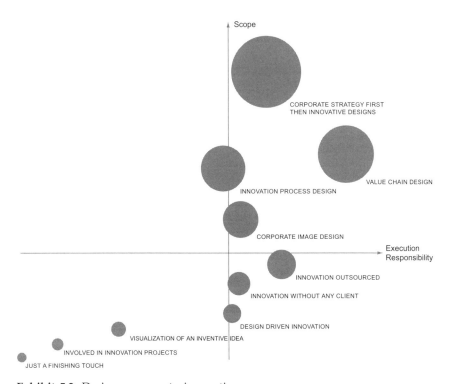

**Exhibit 5.2.** Design avenues to innovation.

As elsewhere,[1] firms in Sweden have transcended the "old" idea of design as simply adding attractive exteriors to products after the development has been concluded, although clients still rely on designers on occasion to give their products a "finishing touch." Increasingly, though, design firms in Sweden are playing a much broader role. Our discussion here helps inform the fuller discussion of design-inspired innovation taken up in subsequent chapters.

In terms of volume of projects, *adding just the finishing touches* remains the foundation for the Swedish industrial design industry. These types of projects typically involve products that are technology-driven, where engineering design or technical features count most. The "finishing touch" may involve greater consciousness for consumer goods that were once largely indistinguishable. "For the Japanese market," one designer explained, "the electronic system should project power and still be small and compact. For other markets, the customer wants a different outer design that suits the local tastes and cultures. We don't get involved in the technology, but are working to make the units easy to service."

We found that all Swedish design firms are seeking to become *involved in innovation projects interactively* with their clients early on. Increasingly, industrial design firms prefer to act as an equal partner in the work to create a product. Designers feel that their broader view can be truly productive in this kind of interactive involvement, even inducing the client to change from one type of material to another or from one manufacturing process to another in an entirely different category.

Industrial designers may serve as a bridge not only between different clients but also between different departments within one client organization. The designers are seen as impartial, engaged at the corporate level, and more likely to understand the different languages of marketing, manufacturing, and research and development. Their concern is for an all-encompassing approach to the entire system.

A third avenue involves designers in refining a promising idea from an inventor through *visualization of the inventive idea*. Most often, designers come up with important additions to the original idea put forth by the inventor. To a large extent, it is this very visualization that allows for improvements. "The inventor is both happy and awed when she first encounters an abstract idea in a 3D-rendering on the computer screen," noted one designer.

Many inventors lack sufficient knowledge about manufacturing or materials, whereas the industrial designer either already has this knowledge or knows where to find it. Some inventors have begun to produce, market, and sell on the basis of the visualizations produced by the design consultancy. Others have succeeded in selling an idea to a company or an investor because the visualization makes the idea look much more "final" than it really is.

We found one very small Swedish industrial design firm specializing entirely in work with inventors. The firm has developed an affordable "service package" aimed at individual inventors; these clients expressed their satisfaction with the service, and some regard the designers as part of a long-term team pursuing the invention.

In many cases, designers begin from dreams and visions. The designer, on her own or prodded by a client, poses a challenging question: "Wouldn't it be great if . . .?" By keeping very close to the frontiers of research and new technology, Swedish design firms find they are in a better position to rely upon new breakthroughs to bring these dreams to fruition. This avenue is *design-driven innovation*, often transcending the original design brief.

Important input to this process is generated most often through keen and unbiased observation of end users while avoiding the potential problems of focus groups or interviews where the user is the captive of an ingrained perception. "We try to uncover the end user's tacit knowledge and silent language," said one designer.

In addition to product design, some firms involve themselves in comprehensive *corporate image design*, including brand, stationery, publications, exhibitions, web design, and more. Here again, the application of a broader perspective is sometimes conducive to innovation. Not all industrial design firms are equipped to offer all-inclusive services, but some do so through a network of suppliers and partners. This type of service can be a step along the way to strategy design (an avenue detailed below).

When engaged in the *value chain design* avenue to innovation, design firms take the lead in evaluating and choosing the materials to be used in an innovative product and finding suppliers for materials, machinery, and possibly sub-contractors for all or part of the manufacturing. This work also takes place for independent inventors; designers refine and elaborate on the inventors' ideas.

*Innovation process design* involves design firms' going beyond design to function also as a management consultancy. Typically, a design consultancy would not be equipped to offer management or organizational design services, but in these types of projects larger firms can play an important role in improving client creativity and helping make the client organization more conducive to design-inspired innovation. In such cases, the design firm may act as a transfer agent between client companies, most often in different industries. We found a very limited number of examples of this type of work in Sweden, but there are examples in other countries. Writing the design manual for a client company might be considered a partial example of this type of work.

Some design firms take on the role of being completely in charge of a client's innovation development. We observe this *innovation contracting* for production-oriented corporations based in Asia that are seeking entry into Western markets or are promoting specialized niches based on their low labor and capital costs. Western companies facing competition from these sources may opt for excellence in ergonomics, for example, and employ expertise from outsider designers to develop entire product lines. Engineering consultancies with design departments are particularly well equipped to undertake the role of product development department "for hire."

When design firms want to see whether some particular expertise they possess could be translated into a marketable product, they may engage in *innovation without a client*. For instance, a firm in the trans-portation cluster that is particularly adept at designing seating for automobiles might translate that expertise into ideas for innovative chairs — and then move forward without a client. We found a specific case in which a Swedish design firm developed an idea that worked and sold the design to a furniture producer. The product was so successful that the designers received follow-up orders for an entire line of chairs. At another firm, a designer challenged himself to come up with a novel concept for a stool with a symmetrical joint that could double as a walking or supporting stick. This product is now exhibited and used by visitors to some 200 museums around the world. At yet another design firm, a lamp was developed that solved a particular problem that a manufacturer had also attempted to address. The industrial designer's solution was smarter. Still another firm prefers so-called "frustration analysis" as its route to the discovery of urgent needs and then to innovation without a client.

### "Frustration Analysis"

Design firms seeking to uncover urgent needs for which they can innovate solutions might select a group of people to keep a diary, for a day or two, of every awkward detail in their daily experiences. It is up to the designers to dig deeper into whatever frustrations might be expressed in these details and look for generalizations, which in turn can be the genesis of innovative designs. The generalization might require a creative leap and even a wholesale change of language (a concept discussed in much greater detail in Chapter 6).

To understand how frustration analysis works, consider the example of a Swedish design firm that was given what seemed like a hopeless assignment. A new skyscraper had too few elevators for the volume of riders during the morning and evening rush hours. People were growing increasingly frustrated with the wait. What could the designers do to fix the problem? The solution was to install mirrors in the elevator lobbies. Frustration disappeared as the riders found something different to occupy their attention. The language had been changed.

We found two Swedish design firms working, to greater or lesser extents, on *corporate strategy followed by innovative design*. First the firms function as management consultants. They address issues of corporate culture, and help establish the client's "identity" based on history, geography, physical factors, and so on. Once established, the identity has to be communicated in products, and the work shifts to design not only of products but also of packaging and even environmental features of the client such as architecture. The designers may also work on product distribution, finding the most appropriate channels for a particular project. Designers engaged in this avenue to innovation are involved in positioning, structuring launches, and resource research.

**How One Swedish Firm Stretches the Concept of Design Services**

Ytterborn & Fuentes (Y&F) offers industrial design services despite employing nearly *no* industrial designers. This is because the firm's scope of service is "corporate identity development." To Y&F, design is seen as but one component in the expression of such identity. So, the firm focuses on long-term strategy; Y&F consultants are strategy experts, and design is seen as an agent for embodying strategies.

In its work, Y&F teams its strategists with the most appropriate specialists for a given project. Sometimes, the team includes Ergonomidesign, Sweden's largest industrial design-only consultancy. In projects, the primary focus is on innovation. To arrive at its innovation strategies, Y&F applies a "strategic filter" with four aspects to understand the client: *genesis* — the client's physical base, history, geographical factors, and so on; *mission* — the very core of the client's business; *products* or, more generally, the client's business offering; and *corporate culture and image.*

One Y&F project was for Hackman, a Finnish company that makes kitchenware. Hackman was heavily dependent on its domestic market (and had captured some 90 percent of Finnish kitchenware sales). An initial strategic decision was to go international, where Hackman was dwarfed by its global competitors. The next step, then, was to establish a distinct Hackman presence by offering a "Formula 1" pan.

Y&F did thorough research long before arriving at the industrial design stage. The consultancy contacted experts on advanced materials at NASA and its spin-offs, plastics materials researchers, and so on. The design brief was very specific and restricting: a unique new materials combination with amazing features, previously unattainable and thus unheard of. Y&F brought in industrial designers from several different countries to design different items within the new kitchenware line — which has garnered more than 50 international design prizes.

Exhibit 5.3 shows the link between the design systems in Sweden discussed earlier and these different avenues to innovation.

**Some lessons**

Industrial designers in Sweden provide a "holistic" view, strive to apply the end user's perspective, and are adept at visualizing. All three factors are conducive to innovation. In addition, industrial designers benefit from technology and impulse transfer between different projects, clients, and industries, and have their clients share this advantage.

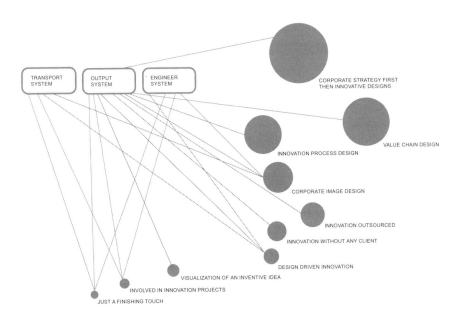

**Exhibit 5.3.** The links between design systems and avenues to innovation in Sweden.

### Design With a Comprehensive Systems View

Three Swedish architecture firms were invited to submit tenders for a waste container station. Two delivered standard, look-alike designs: a building or a high fence. The third has an industrial design group, White Design, and the task was allotted to the designers.

True to their profession, the industrial designers undertook a functional analysis and adopted a comprehensive view of the entire waste management system. What was the basic purpose? What were the different dimensions, aspects, demands? How were the waste containers to be serviced? What were the environmental demands and conditions? How might pests such as rats and birds be kept out? How might the system look after three or eight years? Early research included accompanying the truck drivers as they loaded waste and then unloaded it at existing stations.

White Design suggested, and the customer agreed to, a modular arrangement for movable containers placed within concrete structures. Instead of large trucks, small lorries could be used easily. The aim is to produce no waste (except in the structures) and have no risk of accidents.

All in all, the industrial designers contributed a comprehensive systems viewpoint for solving the client's problem. In fact, they broadened the conception of the end user beyond the waste management client to encompass people who see the site and live near it. In doing so, White Design *delighted* the customer and, to the degree possible when the context is a waste dump, the nearby residents. After all, who would deny that the best waste solution is the one least noticed.

The experience of Swedish design firms suggests several lessons for companies seeking to obtain an advantage in innovation and that rely on industrial design as an important component of the innovation process. While some of the lessons correspond to how Swedish industrial designers tell us *they* would like relationships with clients to work, others coincide with what we know from technology transfer and methods for creative idea generation. One is that companies can benefit from the designer's special facility with brainstorming, functional analysis, broad competencies and experiences, and so on. Similarly, it is advisable to be aware of, and profit from, the power of visualization.

Sweden shows that the "creative friction" that can be generated by engaging multiple design firms offers some potential advantages. For one, access to a larger network of capabilities, solutions, and experience with earlier projects can lead to a larger scope for a design, which may have benefits depending upon the particular project. A larger scope, designers tell us, can result when clients allow designers to sketch scenarios beyond the time horizon of the current project, thus provoking alternatives and sensitivity to longer-term developments that may have value. In this respect, it is best not to short-change the work of designers. The greatest innovative value is realized when designers are engaged early on and permitted to participate all the way through the process, including with last-minute changes or practical adjustments to the product. Advantage from designers' participation accrues best when designers are given sufficient scope.

Why is industrial design more of a force in innovation than it was, say, two decades ago? Globalization has been suggested as one reason, with its concomitant increase in competition and need for adaptation to local cultural habits and alike. Another reason might be the urge to compete in time where the designer's facility for visualization plays a role. Widening the scope has always been a route to innovation, and here industrial design is a fountainhead. Asking fundamental questions and approaching a problem from new and unexpected angles is another such route — again, intelligent ignorance and queries about styling and form may be bliss.

**Tetra Pak**

Ruben Rausing had a vision: "Packaging should save more than its cost." He founded his company, Åkerlund & Rausing, in 1930.

Rausing was influenced by what he saw in the United States, when grocery stores sold prepackaged products — and enjoyed huge efficiency gains. Customers could shop by picking up packaged products themselves rather than having a shop assistant scoop up a certain volume or weight of flour or sugar into a bag. So, Rausing's company developed and produced various packaging systems adapted to individual products. His background in the printing industry was useful since his customers wanted their goods to work as brand statements.

Packaging milk was the ultimate challenge. When he began, milk was poured into light metal containers owned by the customers, who washed and cleaned them for re-use before purchasing more. This "fresh" milk soured quickly.

A more hygienic system — glass bottles — was on the horizon. For a time, this method replaced the pouring at grocery stores. The empty bottles were returned to the shop, which returned them to the dairy to be cleaned and sterilized before re-use. However, glass bottles are fragile and the system was not very efficient. The other alternative at the time, paraffined cartons, didn't work well either.

Rausing tasked his engineers with inventing a packaging system for milk. He believed material such as coated paper or cardboard would work best, but the challenge was to devise and produce a *physical* form.

After playing around with long paper cylinders, a young chemist proposed using a tetrahedron. A topologically inclined mathematician would have known what the Swedish experimenters had discovered: if one presses together a cylinder at two places (perpendicular to each other and also to the axis of the cylinder), the result is a tetrahedron. It is the most elegant way to reduce a round form to four flat triangles. It was the first stroke of genius. Another was the idea that if the closure was *under* the surface of the fluid being packaged, no air could enter — which meant a guarantee of aseptic conditions and that the pasteurized milk would stay fresh much longer. This was an important factor for the entire logistic system, which involved transportation, warehousing, supermarkets, and dairy shops. It was particularly important in places with poor hygienic conditions, including impoverished neighborhoods, developing countries, and places where natural or man-made disasters occurred.

The path to realizing these fine principles was extremely arduous. In his newly created company, Tetra Pak, Rausing's designers still needed to find the best packaging material and the best way to glue the packaging together. Also of concern was that the package would contain *fluid* foodstuff. And what kind of machine could produce the final milk carton with the appropriate brand identity?

Today, ordinary milk cartons are of the Tetra Brik variety. While numerous accessories were developed, from a logistic point of view tetrahedrons were far from ideal. They are still used for special purposes, such as small amounts of cream (or milk), but today the square-angled parallelepiped carton is at a strong advantage. Tetra Brik uses a bit more material than the original tetrahedron, but its form is logistically much more efficient, which leads to other savings. The aseptic principle has been saved, and so the qualities that make for a more sustainable solution that adapts to primitive conditions prevail.

The paper-based milk carton was certainly a step forward from the cumbersome return bottles. But there are some environmental costs: some say that from space one can see a white streak through parts of Asia, a line of empty packaging people have thrown from train cars. Hans Rausing, Ruben's son, started a new venture in an effort to correct this problem. His new company, Ecolean, makes packaging based upon a combination of polymer and chalk, which self-destructs in sunshine and air. The products it can contain vary far more than Tetra Pak. Ukraine is among the early developing markets.

This development trajectory illustrates well the idea of *delight* as part of design-inspired innovation, and shows how delight, excellence, simplicity, and elegance — the terms we introduced in Chapter 1 — must be seen in context. To the mathematically inclined engineer, the tetrahedron that started Tetra Pak is simple and delightful. But it was no delight to consumers, nor to those who had to figure out how to store, transport, and display the odd shape. Tetra Brik may offer a less dramatic geometry, but it evokes delight along the entire logistics chain, including in the milk drinker's refrigerator.

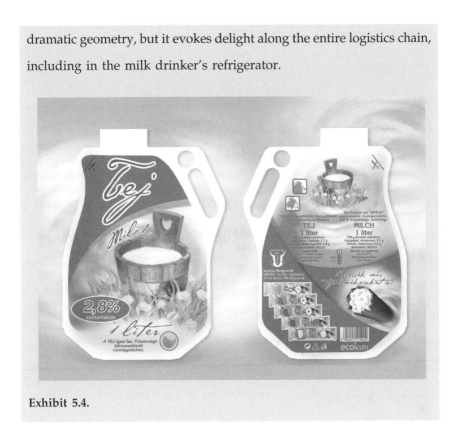

**Exhibit 5.4.**

In Chapter 6, we expand the discussion of the types of work designers engage in for their clients to show how, in the Lombardy region of Italy, a design system has emerged in which design-inspired innovation is becoming a core activity.

**Endnote**

---

[1]B.B. de Mozota, 2004.

# Chapter 6

## *DESIGN-INSPIRED INNOVATION AND THE DESIGN DISCOURSE[1]*

Corporations are looking for an approach for developing products that are not only functionally superior but that also create an emotional link between the product and the consumer. Increasingly, they turn their attention to Italy, especially Lombardy and the area surrounding Milan, where an industry has developed comprising companies that are competing successfully on innovation and value. Alessi, Artemide, and Kartell, among other firms — despite their relatively small size and limited resources — are leading the competition in their industries by creating breakthrough products with superior value. They have achieved their success through a unique recipe.

These successful Italian firms do not consider design as a process to understand and satisfy current user needs, nor as a way to make a product look better. They do not compete simply on style. Rather, these firms see design as an *innovation strategy*. They have developed a unique appro-ach to innovate the deeper emotional and symbolic side of products, to innovate what products mean for people. This "design-inspired inno-vation" has allowed these companies to achieve greater profits and enhanced brand value.

154

"Every market-oriented company has understood that design is an advantage," explains Artemide's Carlotta De Bevilacqua. "Design must not only be the instrument that gives a nice form. Rather it must anticipate a need, proposing a vision."

Italian companies have recognized that they are surrounded by a network of local and global actors — including designers, suppliers, artists, and even firms in other industries — that continuously investigate socio-cultural trends and shape the way people think of and interact with products. This network of actors functions as a huge research laboratory that continuously experiments, proposes new products and broader choices for consumers, selects new ideas, and promotes new values. The laboratory comprises thousands of interactions and both formal and informal cooperation among institutions, firms, and professionals. This *design discourse* is a diffused dialog on possible new design languages and meanings. Italian manufacturers are leveraging this design discourse to propose and realize design-inspired innovations.

Understanding the approach to innovation of successful Italian firms is not an easy task. However, a framework for interpreting the peculiar nature of this innovation strategy will help, and will allow us to discuss how this strategy is supported by the design discourse.

## Design as innovation of meanings

What is design-inspired innovation and how does it lead to competitive advantage? To highlight the peculiar approach of Italian manufacturers requires taking the widely acknowledged definition of design as the integrated innovation of function and form and adapting it further to the framework illustrated in Exhibit 6.1.

The classic dialectic of function versus form leads designers to relegate the latter to the aesthetic appearance of products; indeed, the debate often focuses simplistically on the contrast between functionalism/rationalism and styling — particularly in the context of industries where aesthetic content is deemed to drive competition (such as furniture and lighting). Exhibit 6.1 expands and elaborates the concept of form to capture better the communicative and semantic dimension of products.

As many designers know, a product's aesthetic appearance (its style) is but one of many ways it can bring messages to the user. What really matters to the user, in addition to functionality, is a product's emotional and symbolic value — its *meaning*. If functionality aims at satisfying the

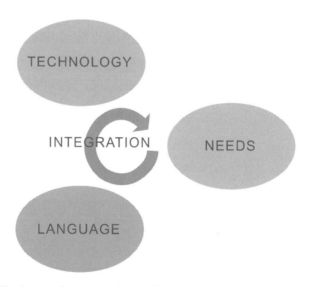

**Exhibit 6.1.** Design as the generation and integration of knowledge. Adapted from Verganti, 2003.

operative needs of the customers, the product meaning tickles their emotional and socio-cultural needs. Product meaning proposes to users a system of values, a personality and identity, that may easily go beyond style.[2] As Krippendorff has written, "The etymology of design goes back to the Latin *de* + *signare* and means making something, distinguishing it by a sign, giving it significance, designating its relation to other things, owners, users or goods. Based on this original meaning, one could say: design is making sense (of things)."[3] This interpretation of design, evident to design managers who also deal strategically with brand identity and communication, actually reflects the dictionary definition of the word design: "to indicate with a distinctive mark, sign or name."[4]

The example of the lamp Metamorfosi by Artemide illustrates this perspective. Artemide, founded by Ernesto Gismondi and Sergio Mazza in 1959, is a leading high-end Italian lighting manufacturer. The company is highly regarded for its designs and counts several products in prominent museums. In 1998, Artemide launched its first Metamorfosi release, comprising several products of which Exhibit 6.2 is an example. (Exhibits 6.3 and 6.4 show Metamorfosi in more detail.)

Metamorfosi is the result of an innovation of *meanings*. It is based on the concept of a Human Light. Not a traditional lamp, it is a system to produce light, particularly colored light, that can be customized according to the specific emotional needs of the user. Here light is deemed as responsible for emotional conditions, thoughts, and memories, and is therefore intimately connected with people's wellbeing. A user likely buys this lamp not because of its "nice" style but because of its "nice" light.

The system consists of a novel patented technology, based on a small electronic control system that allows the user (through a remote-control panel) to create and memorize several color atmospheres (combinations of monochromatic lights and haloes) generated by three parabolic reflectors equipped with dichroic filters.

*Source:* Mentamorfosi Yang, Artemide, Design by Carlotta De Bevilacqua, 2000.

**Exhibit 6.2.** Metamorfosi by Artemide.

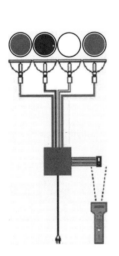

**Exhibit 6.3.** The Metamorfosi "tool kit".

**Exhibit 6.4.** How the Metamorfosi lamp lights a room.

Artemide's innovation of meaning — buying light instead of lamps — is evident. The designers underline this innovation by minimizing the forms and using translucent materials, thus hiding the physical object, and in turn giving greater value to the real message delivered by the product: the emotions evoked by its light.

The Metamorfosi example also illustrates how a given meaning is achieved by using a specific design *language* — that is, the set of signs, symbols, and icons (of which style is just an instance) designers can adopt to deliver the message. Translucency and minimalism of the object, for example, is the language of Metamorfosi to express the sense of human light.

The Human Light vision became the strategic driver of the entire company mission, in an industry where product style and appearance are generally the drivers of competition. Several competitors are imitating Artemide by working on light colors and on the sense of wellbeing produced by light. Artemide, meanwhile, is continuously moving ahead by innovating the system.

**Giving meaning to design**

In the Exhibit 6.1 framework, innovation may concern a product's functional utility, its design language, or both. Functional innovation may imply an incremental or wholesale improvement of technical performance. Innovation in the semantic dimension may similarly be more or less radical. For instance, a product may adopt a language and deliver a message that is in line with current socio-cultural models or that follows the evolution of existing and established trends. Since the product would conform to existing definitions of beauty, users would probably perceive it as stylish. This *incremental* approach to innovation of product meanings usually occurs when companies ask their designers to provide an engineered product with an appealing look. The objective in design terms is to design a style that conforms to accepted existing languages.

In other cases, a product may adopt a language and deliver a message that implies a significant reinterpretation of its meaning. Users would give to this product a very new meaning. Artemide's Metamorfosi is an example of such innovation of meaning. The users no longer search for a beautiful lamp, but rather for a light that makes them feel better.

A reinterpretation of meaning is not necessarily immediate; it takes time. Users need to understand the new language and message, find new connections to their socio-cultural context, and explore new symbolic values and patterns of interaction with the product.

As with technological innovations that demand profound changes in technological regimes,[5] innovations of meaning demand profound changes in socio-cultural regimes. We are not referring to "fashionable" or stylish products here, but rather to products that may contribute to the definition of new design languages and that might become "fashionable" in the future. Sales of such products may not soar rapidly, but increase more slowly. They are stable and long-lasting. A firm pursuing this approach sees design as a driver of change rather than as a tool to give a nice form to objects, and is placing design at the heart of its competitive strategy.

Successful Italian manufacturers in design-intensive industries have demonstrated unique capabilities to master design-inspired innovation. Their innovation strategy couples several incremental projects with punctuated attempts to introduce *breakthrough* changes of product meanings. These breakthroughs explore routes, move the frontier of design languages, set new standards of interpretation, and satisfy latent needs and desires. Through design-inspired innovations, the breakthroughs stand as landmarks of innovation in their industries, and therefore create high brand value that allows them to overtake their competitors.

Alessi's well-known product line "Family follows fiction" — a set of colored plastic kitchenware products filled with irony, provocation, and a childlike quality — is another compelling example of design-inspired innovation. Alessi conceived this product line in 1991, when no one thought that kitchenware could be anything but functional products made of steel. The company was among the first to recognize and explore the emotional side of consumption. Today, several firms now follow a similar path, both within and outside Alessi's industry, and even scholars advocate the emotional and experiential dimension of products.[6] Meanwhile, Alessi has created and maintains a strong competitive position as a global leader in a highly competitive market.

Another example of design-inspired innovation is the famous "Bookworm" bookshelf by Kartell (see Exhibit 6.5), a personalized painting

*Source:* Designed by Ron Arad, 1994.

**Exhibit 6.5.** Kartell Bookworm.

of written knowledge and culture rather than a functional place to store books. A highly successful product, some 250,000 Bookworm units were sold in the 10 years after the product launch.

These products are good, straightforward examples that illustrate the various elements of the definition of design-inspired innovation we offered in Chapter 1. They are simple and elegant; they delight their users; they create meaning; and, in the case of the Human Light, they are innovative at the systems level.

**Pursuing design-inspired innovation**

A growing number of companies recognize the importance of design-inspired innovation, especially those that aim to strengthen and maintain a high brand value. These companies are willing to take the large risks associated with this quite complex and uncertain approach. How can a firm achieve a design-inspired innovation? How can it define new meanings that are successful in the marketplace? To answer these questions, let us first look generally at innovation as the result of a process of generation and integration of knowledge.[7] Where does this knowledge come from when dealing with design-inspired innovation?

As mentioned in Chapter 1, three types of knowledge are essential for an innovation process: knowledge about user needs; knowledge about technological opportunities; and knowledge about product languages. The last component concerns the signs that can be used to deliver a message to the user and the semantic context (socio-cultural models) in which the user will give meaning to those signs (e.g., the symbols, indexes, and icons a designer might choose to deliver a message of a "human light" to the user). Exhibit 6.6 illustrates the role of these three types of knowledge in design-inspired innovation and contrasts this strategy with two other typical situations: technology-push innovation, where innovation emerges from the availability of new technology principles and devices; and market-pull (or user-centered[8])

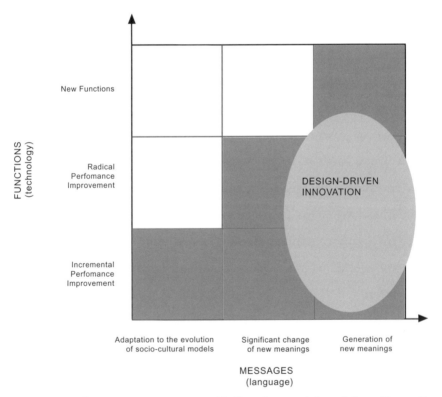

**Exhibit 6.6.** The innovation strategy of Italian firms. Adapted from Verganti, 2003.

innovation, where innovation answers more or less explicit and immediate customer needs.[9] Exhibit 6.6 illustrates the positioning of these three types of innovations within the framework.

Knowledge about a product language is present in all three situations. In fact, as Exhibit 6.6 shows, innovation of function and message occurs in any novel project. However, what is remarkably different across the three situations is the role played by this type of knowledge. The major drivers of innovation in market-pull and technology-push endeavors are knowledge about user needs and knowledge about technology, respectively. In these two cases, knowledge about product language usually enters the innovation process along the way as ancillary knowledge.

Design-inspired innovation — that is, an innovation that proposes breakthrough messages — has a completely different balance among the three types of knowledge. Here the driver of innovation, the starting point, is neither technology (although technology is crucial as a means to create new meanings) nor a customer requirement. It is difficult to imagine that a user would ever explicitly ask for a "human light" or for a flexible spiraliform bookshelf or for a spaceship-like squeezer (Alessi's famous Juicy Salif lemon squeezer by Philippe Starck). The firms that created these products rarely rely on classic market analysis based on surveys or focus groups, nor do they invest intensively in the ethnographic research techniques that have been getting so much attention in the business arena. These firms know that they would never achieve a far-reaching innovation of meanings from these methods, since a *radical* innovation of meaning is not pulled by the market. Rather, it results from a vision about a *possible* future.

Ernesto Gismondi, chairman of Artemide, explains: "We make *proposals* to people." Alberto Alessi, CEO of the company that bears his name, supports this view: "Working within the metaproject *transcends the creation of an object purely to satisfy a function and necessity.* Each object represents a tendency, a *proposal* and an indication of progress which has a more *cultural* resonance." Behind these words we find the ambition to be a driver of change in society, or at least to increase — through the company offering — the probability that the world will change to some degree in a direction closer to the system of values and beliefs of the entrepreneur.

These "proposals" by Italian manufacturers are not dreams without a foundation. In one way or another, these design-push proposals eventually satisfy future user needs and lead to great market success. How do these companies manage to make innovative proposals that are also profitable? How do they create breakthrough messages — those that eventually emerge as the messages that users were looking for (even if they were looking subconsciously)?

## The design discourse

The meaning a user gives to a product depends on the user's cognitive model, which, in turn, is significantly affected by his or her socio-cultural context. Proposing new product meanings implies understanding the *inner* dynamics of socio-cultural models, beyond what is explicitly visible nowadays.

Italian manufacturers have developed an exceptional capability to *understand*, *anticipate*, and *influence* the emergence of new product meanings. They ignore bandwagons, and instead search for new design languages by looking at those socio-cultural phenomena that are currently less perceivable, but that will be the trends of tomorrow and the likely reality of the future. They *detect* the whispers in the current socio-cultural models, *identify* the weak voices likely to grow stronger in the future, *select* among them those whispers that most match their own values, and *help* these voices become understandable and meaningful through their new product offering.

The process through which Italian manufacturers develop knowledge about possible future socio-cultural evolutions and formulate new product meanings is difficult to track. Knowledge about the subtle and unexpressed dynamics of socio-cultural models is not written in books. This knowledge is not codified, but is *tacit* and implicit. It has to be sought out and developed through a continuous process. It is not found in sociological scenarios of the future, which usually describe *dominant* trends and are *extrapolations* of current phenomena. What books and reports on the future describe is usually already known to the most advanced firms. Design-inspired innovation assumes that a firm's proposals will be a *modification* of the scenario.

Further, this knowledge is *distributed*; it cannot be retrieved from a single repository. The shaping of socio-cultural models and their impact on the interpretation of product languages depends on millions of unpredictable interactions between users, firms, designers, products, communication media, cultural centers, schools, artists, and so on — as studies of how culture is produced have shown.[10] In other words, a firm is immersed in a network of actors who both explore future meanings and, with their actions, influence the creation of new cultural models.

Consider Artemide as an example. The company's challenge is to understand what people will delight in as they live in their homes. In other words, they are searching for possible future domestic mindsets and lifestyles that can be addressed by new proposals. Artemide finds itself surrounded by other actors facing the same challenge: firms in other home-living industries (such as manufacturers of furniture, small appliances, TV sets, etc.) that are willing to propose design-inspired innovations; product designers that provide new projects for these manufacturers; interior design magazines and other media that often develop domestic scenarios; suppliers of raw materials interested in how their new materials might be used in household products; universities and design schools, where professors and students conduct workshops to design domestic products; and showroom and exhibition designers that explore new spatial organization.

These actors are all interested in understanding possible future domestic scenarios. They all carry on research into these scenarios and all develop knowledge about socio-cultural models. Through their actions and outputs (products, projects, reports, shows, etc.) they influence what people will actually think and love about living in their homes. Interacting with these actors increases the capability to understand and influence socio-cultural models and, therefore, increases the probability of developing deep-seated innovations of meanings that will be highly successful in the future marketplace.

Italian manufacturers place high value on their interactions with this network of actors, whom they consider to be *interpreters* of the evolution of future scenarios with whom to share their own visions, exchange information on trends, and test the robustness of their assumptions. What these manufacturers have understood is that knowledge about socio-cultural models is diffused within their external environment. They see themselves as immersed in a huge research laboratory that includes the investigations and interactions of designers, firms, artists, and schools. This networked laboratory is the *design discourse* — a continuous dialog on socio-cultural models (foreseen and desired) and their implications for patterns of consumption, meanings, and product languages, occurring through explicit and tacit interactions among several actors both in the global and local setting.

It is interesting to note that similar attention to research processes outside a firm is also occurring in *technological* innovation.[11] Recent studies have shown that firms should manage research and development in a systemic perspective, where their R&D lab, albeit large, is only a small part of a huge network of researchers, institutions and firms. Scholars, in this context, speak of Business Ecosystems[12] or Open Innovation.[13] Von Hippel has further investigated the crucial role of users in these networks of innovators.[14] This phenomenon is even more relevant when considering innovation of languages, since socio-cultural models are really shaped outside into society and internal R&D labs can only detect and influence them.

The Italian manufacturers we studied understand how to leverage the design discourse to propose innovations of meanings. They recognize that an important part of their competitive advantage rests on their ability to access and influence the design discourse as a crucial carrier to their users. These manufacturers have developed unique practices that allow them to identify the key interpreters in the design discourse, attract them and develop a privileged relationship, share some information while keeping control of their own unique vision, and use the design discourse to communicate with users.

The design discourse in Milan is particularly rich and intense, and local companies have the opportunity to exploit a localization advantage for easier and deeper interaction with interpreters. Several furniture manufacturers there have developed a superior capability to propose design-inspired innovations.

## The design discourse in the Milan system

In Lombardy, the design discourse unfolds among participants spread throughout the world, who interact by exchanging knowledge on socio-cultural models — but local networks and local dialogs are crucial. The whisperings of the design discourse diffuse through personal relations, cooperation in workshops and projects, and informal interactions. The quality of the dialog benefits substantially from geographical proximity and, for a manufacturer, being close to a region or an area where the design discourse is advanced offers a significant advantage. Indeed, the quality of the design discourse in Italy, and especially in Lombardy (the region of which Milan is the capital), is a major contributor to the success of many local manufacturers of products for the home.

Milan is widely regarded as one of the worldwide capitals of design.[15] The city of 1.5 million is the center of an articulated system of actors dealing with design, the borders of which encompass the entire Lombardy region — also one of the most advanced and industrialized regions in Italy and one of the core industrial and cultural settings in Europe.[16]

The Milan Design System operates in several product categories, but the core competencies of design in Milan focus on two specific contexts of use: domestic products (including furniture, lighting, kitchens, household items, small appliances, white goods, kitchenware, and so on) and goods for personal style (such as clothing and textile products, jewelry, and fashion accessories). Design activity is most intense in the first category.

Note that we use the term design "system" rather than "district" or "industrial cluster", both terms more commonly found in the literature.[17] The Milan Design System is neither the cluster of design firms and consultants in Milan, nor is it the cluster of Lombardy furniture manufacturers. Both clusters are *elements* of the entire system, which encompasses other elements that are concerned with and benefit from interaction with the local design discourse. For example, Lombardy is home to the design centers of many automobile manufacturers, as design languages for the interior of cars and their body styling are strongly interrelated with that of homes. The system includes suppliers of raw materials (Italian furniture is well known for its advanced use of new polymers and other new materials instead of wood), sub-contractors, and so on. We do not speak of an industrial cluster because many of the actors do not belong to industry: major players in the Milan Design System also include the universities and design schools, museums, showrooms, service providers (photographers, advertising agencies, etc.), craftsmen, publishers of architectural and interior design magazines, exhibitors and fairs, and artists. Exhibit 6.7 shows the Milan Design System and the design discourse that takes place within the system.

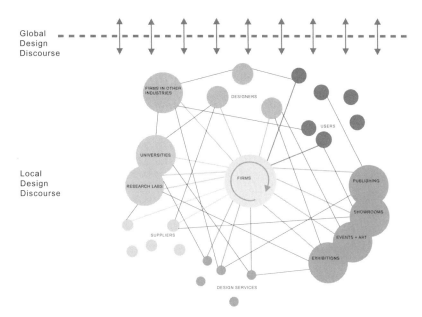

Global
Design
Discourse

Local
Design
Discourse

FIRMS IN OTHER
INDUSTRIES

DESIGNERS

USERS

UNIVERSITIES

FIRMS

PUBLISHING

RESEARCH LABS

SHOWROOMS

SUPPLIERS

EVENTS + ART

EXHIBITIONS

DESIGN SERVICES

**Exhibit 6.7.** Actors in the Lombardy design system.

This system is complex, multifaceted, and has permeable borders. Exhibit 6.8 summarizes the basic characteristics of the major actors in the design discourse in Milan and provides benchmarking figures where available.

As Exhibit 6.8 shows, the local community that deals with design — and especially with domestic lifestyle — is rich and dense. However, what makes the Milan Design System special is not the quality and number of individual actors, but rather the quality of their interactions. In other words, what makes the local design discourse unique is not the nodes of the network, but the *linkages*. In Lombardy, links between manufacturers and designers are especially strong. This strength of

| Actor | Characteristics |
|---|---|
| Manufacturers of domestic products | Overall turnover of Italian manufacturers is 54 billion euros (of which 54% are exports). Italy is the largest world exporter of furniture (16%, Germany is second with 8%). Lombardy accounts for 23% of Italian furniture manufacturers and 20% of employees. (data from 2000). These are mostly small and medium enterprises (average size is 8 employees per firm). <br> Several firms are positioned in the high-end segments of the market. They adopt and combine several technologies and materials (not only wood). Most do not have a design department, but have strategic marketing, branding, engineering, and R&D. Ideas and concepts often come from outside (designers), but technology and brand are strongly controlled internally. |
| Design firms | 700 design firms in Milan (60% of total Italian design industry). Mainly micro-firms and studios (30% are individual professionals, 77% have less then 4 employees, only 1 firm over 100 employees). Many designers have a degree in architecture. Many foreign designers. 90% of these design firms have done projects with domestic products. 69% have also done projects in other fields. Most designers specialize in concept generation. They do not have engineering capability (do not provide a full product development service). |
| Users | Italian families spend about 10% of their non-food budget on furniture products, more than in any other European country. Lombardy has about 16% of Italian population but about 21% of Italian purchasing of domestic products. Local users are quite literate on domestic lifestyle, being themselves immersed in the design discourse. |
| OEMs in other industries | Lombardy is the most advanced industrial setting in Italy and one of the main manufacturing and research territories in Europe. There are a wide variety of industrial sectors, with no special major focus. Several multinational corporations have located their design centers in Milan. |
| Suppliers | Several small and medium size suppliers upstream in the furniture supply chain (suppliers of components, assemblies, production technologies, etc.). They are geographically concentrated, and are highly specialized, with a great flexibility with respect to demand and innovation (see the study of Piore and Sabel 1984) |
| Support Services | Milan has a high density of support services for design-inspired innovation, such as advertisement agencies (38% of Italy, of which 85% operates in industries related to domestic products) and PR agencies (79% of Italy, of which 36% focus on design activities). There is still a considerable number of craftsmen who are prone to experimentation and to producing small lots of units and prototypes for manufacturers. |
| Associations | Milan hosts the Italian Association for Design (whose 750 members are professional designers) and the Italian Association of furniture manufacturers (the largest in Europe). |
| Schools, Universities, Research centers | Milan is a worldwide center for architecture and design education. Politecnico di Milano, the oldest Italian university in these fields, enrolls each year about 2,000 graduates in architecture (about 30% of Italian architectural students) and 900 graduates in design (more than 60% of graduate Italian design students). Politecnico di Milano also offer the only Italian PhD program in design. Significant interaction with the professional environment: more than 60% of lecturers are designers or professionals with their own design activity. <br> Other internationally known non-university schools are Domus Academy, Instituto Europeo del Design, NABA, Scuola Politecnica del Design. |
| Fairs | Each April, Milan hosts the most important international furniture fair: the Salone del Mobile. The entire city is the center of events, seminars, and so on under the name of the "Milano Design Week", attracting people from all over the world. In 2003, 170,000 firms presented their products at the fair, and 3,300 journalists attended (50% from abroad). |
| Exhibitions | The "Triennale di Milano" has been the Italian cultural center for architecture, design, and modern art since the early 1920s. <br> 57% of firms specializing in exhibition design are located in Milan. <br> Many Milan showrooms (especially in the domestic and fashion industries) experiment with new languages and signs. |
| Publishers | Milan hosts 756 publishers (25% of Italian publishers). About 60% of them are active in the field of design. <br> There are 16 design magazines published in Milan, 10 of which are published in English and have international distribution. |

*Source:* Adapted from Verganti and Dell'Era, 2003 and Bertola *et al.,* 2002.

**Exhibit 6.8.** Characteristics of the actors in the Lombardy design system.

Lombardy corresponds directly to what policymakers have deemed to be the crucial factor. Indeed, other European areas place "improving interaction between manufacturers and designers" as the most important goal of their design policy among thirteen possible objectives (followed by "improving design management practices" and "promoting the strategic role of design among manufacturers").[18] Foreign policymakers look to Lombardy as a model for the development of design in their regions.

Italian manufacturers demonstrate their recognition of the importance and value of the local design discourse through their nurture and support. In the 1980s, a cultural movement known as Memphis revolutionized the world of design by proposing a breakthrough language based on bold patterns, daring colors, and plastic laminate surfaces. Memphis delivered a message of irony and provocation that contrasted with the peaceful conformity of the decade's so-called "good" design. When Ettorre Sottsass, the movement's leader, needed funding to launch this avant-garde initiative, he went to Artimede chairman Ernesto Gismondi, who provided the money. Artemide recognized that Memphis was a research laboratory to explore new languages. "For me," says Gismondi, "this was an experiment."

Of course, creating a rich design discourse is no easy task. It requires considerable time and the coordinated actions of several actors. The good news is that a local design discourse takes place in every region, because discussion of socio-cultural models occurs everywhere. Bringing this discussion into the production and industrial context may take time, but it also creates virtuous cycles: the more well developed a region's design discourse, the more that region attracts talent and investments from beyond, and the more it attracts the more it becomes attractive. This explains why Italy, despite suffering a brain drain in many technological disciplines, benefits from brain attraction in design. Many products of Italian manufacturers are designed by non-Italians working in Lombardy. As the well-known Israeli designer Ron Arad has said, "Northern Italy is the center of the design world, not just because of the design that comes from Italy, but, above all, because of its manufacturing culture; there is no other place in the world where you can find such a vast array of manufacturers who know the value of design."

### Involving designers as brokers of languages

The greatest strength of the design system in Lombardy is in the interaction between manufacturers and designers. Italian manufacturers develop design-inspired innovation by leveraging an external network of interpreters that participate in the design discourse. What is the process by which these manufacturers involve external designers in their innovation process?

Italian firms recognize that design consultants may act as focal actors in the design system. They are a crucial access point to the design discourse and therefore to the discussions that are going to shape the future of product meanings. In other words, designers may act as gatekeepers in the evolving flow of socio-cultural models. They are brokers of knowledge on design languages.

The idea of designers as *brokers* of knowledge is not new. A 1997 study of IDEO showed how this famous design firm acts as a *technology* broker, having access to as many as 40 different industries and exploiting its network position to move solutions across industries.[19] What is peculiar in design-inspired innovation is that designers act as brokers of knowledge about *languages* rather than technology. Of course, technological competence is still crucial (as a means of speaking new languages), but the greatest value comes from their ability to understand the subtle dynamics of values and meanings in society and the impact these have on product language. They facilitate their manufacturing clients' access to the ongoing discussion about these dynamics and languages. They bring bits of knowledge, helping their clients interpret the design discourse, and position themselves in this discourse.

Knowledge about languages is key here. Designers do not act as sociologists. They may talk about hidden and emerging phenomena in the society, but more often they talk about new, unexpressed, semantic needs of users. They *observe* the socio-cultural models and make *proposals* to affect the emerging dynamics in socio-cultural models. Their attitudes are more reminiscent of *architects* (indeed, most designers Italian manufacturers involve in their innovation strategies hold architecture degrees). Architects design buildings — products that usually survive the customer. Architects are accustomed to looking beyond immediate needs, having a vision about an unexpressed future, and proposing signs that inevitably modify our context.

Another difference between designers and sociologists is that the involvement of designers is pragmatic. Designers apply their knowledge to products. Hence, more than talking about socio-cultural models, they speak of product meanings and languages, of product signs that are moving and spreading across different contexts.

Product languages are not industry-specific: they move across industries even more fluently than does technology. Consider, for example, the diffusion of colored translucent materials from home furnishings to computers — a linguistic exercise that allowed the Apple iMac to speak the language of the home rather than the office. Further, design languages move across different socio-cultural worlds (e.g., across different countries). This is a more complex process than the fertilization of signs across industries. The embedding of meanings in culture is significant. Precisely for this reason, a global corporation willing to propose an innovation of meanings needs to access knowledge on design languages beyond the borders of its socio-cultural context. Hence, like technology brokers, designers exploit their network position to move languages (and the meaning and values attached by people) across industries and socio-cultural worlds. By doing so, they support the creation of new meanings that simultaneously have a socio-cultural foundation. Indeed, Italian manufacturers involve a great deal of foreign designers in their innovation process, combining and integrating the brokering of knowledge in both the local and the global setting.

How might a corporation effectively involve designers in its own innovation process and profit from their brokering capabilities? The example of the Metamorfosi innovation process (see box) provides some excellent insights and helps identify some general guidelines. One is to *involve design consultants early in the innovation process*. A peculiarity of Artemide's approach was the intense involvement of designers in the first macro-phase: research on new languages. This research process is where the seeds of design-inspired innovation are first planted, where understanding meanings and languages provides maximum strategic impact, and where the role of designers as brokers of languages has its maximum value.

Another guideline is to *have brokers of languages talking with top managers*. As a strategy to build long-term competitive advantage, design-inspired innovation demands direct involvement of senior executives. The process of research on new languages is rooted in interactions between executives and designers, as the Artemide example shows. Given that designers act on the strategic resources of a corporation (its system of values and the messages it bring to users), they are functioning as strategic consultants. Unlike traditional strategic analysis, however, the process of research in languages is based on discussions. It cannot be squeezed into a report or a study. The interaction between executives and designers implies a significant investment of management time.

It is important to *involve design consultants according to their ability to broker knowledge*. Knowledge on languages is not codified or developed through methods but is diffused throughout a complex network of actors.

Designers should be selected according to their capability to access this network, connect local and global languages, and broker signs across a wide range of industries. You should value your designers' knowledge more than their creativity and tools.

Similarly important, *select design consultants according to shared values.* Design-inspired innovation implies proposing new meanings where a firm projects its own values to change the environment. Design consultants, on the other hand, have their own path of research on the dynamics of socio-cultural models, and have their own systems of values. We have highlighted above the similarity between the attitude of top Italian executives and the attitude of designers: both of them are design-pushed and are driven by visions and ideology. When their research paths cross, ideas may contrast, but basic values need to be aligned. They cannot be adapted to suit a particular client or designer.

Several other guidelines emerge from the Milan Design System. For instance, it is key to *nurture your long-term relationships with the design consultants you involve in design-inspired innovation.* This process demands trust, and trust requires time and long-term cooperation. Related to this point about relationships is that companies and designers should *talk beyond contracts.* The exchange of tacit and diffused knowledge, access to the design discourse, sharing of values, and development of trust are all activities that cannot be restricted within the rigid walls of contracts between the client and the design consultant. Research on languages is a continuous process. It occurs outside typical space and timeframes, and only occasionally takes the explicit form described in the Artemide's example. It requires an intimate relationship that goes beyond contracts. Indeed, most top executives of leading Italian manufacturers combine professional and personal relations with their design consultants.

*Do not talk only with your design consultants*; they are but one of several channels to access knowledge on languages. Artemide, for example, cooperates with design schools, promotes cultural events, engages in studies on socio-cultural trends, discusses with managers and experts, and participates in direct dialog with its customers.

It is best to *develop your own research path*. Design consultants should be considered gatekeepers: they provide an easier access to knowledge that otherwise would be difficult to grasp. They cannot substitute for the internal research process through which a firm develops its own vision. A firm may contract for product development, but not the development of its values and meanings. A firm that lacks the inner capability to develop knowledge on languages will hardly be able to understand and embed contributions from brokers of languages.

### The Innovation Process of Artemide Metamorfosi

Artemide's process to develop the Metamorfosi system comprised three macro-phases. The first was *research on new languages*, which drove the entire endeavor. In 1995 Artemide was exploring new systems of values to strengthen its market leadership position, which was under threat from new global competitors. Several approaches were used to access knowledge on new systems of values and product languages. A core part of this process was a workshop that involved founder and CEO Ernesto Gismondi, his wife Carlotta De Bevilacqua (Artemide's managing director for brand strategy and development direction), five well-known designers, and a design professor. A doctor and a psychologist coordinated the workshop, which explored new meanings of light in context of people's biological, psychological, and cultural spheres. The result was the creation of the vision of Human Light.

The second macro-phase involved *research on new technologies*. Directed by the R&D department, the firm searched for technologies to express the new meanings of Human Light. This led to the development of a basic "technology kit," including the dichroic filters and the computer for controlling the lamps and customizing/memorizing different light scenarios (the technology kit was eventually sold as a separate product).

*Product development*, the third macro-phase, involved integrating new languages and technologies into products. Here Artemide provided different designers with the basic message (the Human Light) and the technology kit and asked them to develop lamps based on the Metamorfosi concept. Some of these designers had already participated in the research phase; others were new to the project. In this phase, the focus of languages moved from meanings and messages to the form of the object.

The guidelines to involve designers have a basic principle: brokering of design languages is not a service that can be easily bought in the consulting market. Ultimately, the very approach a company takes to involve designers is itself a source of competitive advantage, as demonstrated by leading Italian manufacturers. This approach needs to be built over time by combining three unique ingredients: a personal network of long-term relationships with brokers of languages, an entire array of alternative channels that complement and enrich the access to this knowledge, and an internal process to integrate all contributions. Only the unique, firm-specific combination of these factors will lead to sustainable, not imitable, competitive advantage.

Often, large corporations underestimate the importance of interaction with the design discourse, or delegate this task to specific departments in the firm, thus restraining top executives from direct contact. The Italian manufacturers' approach is quite the opposite: the founder or CEO is *directly* immersed. The companies make a long-term investment in design-inspired innovation. They work to maintain the capability to develop vision and select the best path, and make sure it is not buried beneath layers of organization.

In Chapter 7, we explore in more detail the close link between design, the understanding of meaning in a product, and the creation of a product language. Our laboratory for that exploration is a product full of meaning — the *wheelchair*.

**Endnotes**

---

[1] A substantially more detailed discussion of the topics discussed in this chapter can be found in R. Verganti, 2003.

[2] Research in marketing and consumer behavior has demonstrated that the affective/emotional and symbolic/sociocultural dimension of consumption is as important as the utilitarian perspective of classic economic models, even for industrial clients. See M. Csikszentmihalyi, 2003; S. Fournier, 1991; R.E. Kleine III,

S.S. Kleine and J.B. Kernan, 1993; H. Mano and R.L. Oliver, 1993; S. Brown, 1995; D. Holt, 1997; D. Holt, 2003; S. Bhat and S.K. Reddy, 1998; E. Fischer, 2000; M.T. Pham, J.B. Cohen, J.W. Pracejus and G.D. Hughes, 2001; A. Oppenheimer 2005; S.-P. Tsai, 2005. The semantic dimensions of design have been actually recognized and underlined also by several design scholars and theorists: V. Margolin and R. Buchanen (eds.), 1995; R. Cooper and M. Press, 1995; T.-M. Karjalainen, 2003.

[3]K. Krippendorff, 1989.

[4]*Merriam-Webster's Collegiate Dictionary, 10th Ed.*, Merriam-Webster, Inc, Springfield, MA, 1993.

[5]B. Latour, 1987; M. Callon, 1991; W. Bijker and J. Law (eds.), 1994; F.W. Geels, 2004.

[6]B. Schmitt, 1999; D.A. Norman, 2004.

[7]M. Iansiti, 1998. Others have looked at the innovation processes of firms from a resource-based perspective. See B. Wernerfelt, 1984; B. Kogut and U. Zander, 1992; K.R. Conner and C.K. Prahalad, 1996.

[8]User-centered innovation implies the development of new products starting from a deep analysis of user behaviors in the context of use. It adopts advanced user analysis methods such as applied ethnography that can support the discovery of unarticulated needs from users. It is a quite advanced innovation approach that has recently attracted considerable attention both from practitioners (B. Nussbaum, 2004) and scholars (T. Kelley, 2001; K. Vredenburg, S. Isensee and C. Righi, 2002; V. Kumar and P. Whitney, 2003; Lojacono and Zaccai, 2004; R.W. Veryzer and B.B. de Mozota, 2005). We consider user-centered innovation to be a market-pull approach because it postulates the basic hypothesis that users can directly or indirectly suggest directions for innovation, and therefore that innovation processes should start from users as they currently think and act, and therefore from their current needs. As such, this approach tends to be more incremental as it searches for unmet needs in the existing socio-cultural regime.

[9] The debate on market-pull versus technology-push innovation is as old as the debate on the definition of design (for a theory and critique, see G. Dosi, 1982). Simplified categories are used here to stimulate a reflection on the peculiarities of design-inspired innovation.

[10]R.A. Peterson and N. Anand, 2004.

[11]O. Sorenson and D.M. Waguespack, 2005.

[12]M. Iansiti and R. Levien, 2004.

[13]H.W. Chesbrough, 2003.

[14]Eric von Hippel, 2005.

[15]See, for example, J.K. Galbraith, 1997.

[16]Lombardy has a population of about 9 million (i.e., 15.9 percent of the total Italian population). Intra-muros research investments in Lombardy amount

to 2.8 billion euros, which is some 22.5 percent of Italian R&D investments, one-third of Italian private (business) R&D investments, and about 50 percent of the EPO patents (ISTAT 1999). Thus, industrial and research activity in Lombardy is comparable to that of some entire European nations, including Finland, Ireland, Sweden, Belgium, and Denmark.

[17]M.J. Piore and C.F. Sabel, 1984; M. Porter, 1990.

[18]A study of design policies (R. Verganti and C. Dell'Era, 2003) has compared and benchmarked the strengths and weaknesses of local design discourses in the main European design systems: Catalonia (Spain), Denmark, Finland, Lombardy, London, Rhone-Alps (France), and Sweden. While all are different in that some are regions, others nations, and still others metropolitan areas, all are of similar size and reach, and are the focus of policies aimed at developing investment in design. In the study, a panel of 26 international experts and observers were asked to assess the quality of nodes and links of these systems through a Delphi process.

[19]See A.B. Hargadon and R.I. Sutton, 1997; P. Bertola and J.C. Texeira, 2003, which also provide an interesting study of designers as knowledge brokers that investigates the role of designers by comparing 15 case studies of large corporations from the Design Management Institute collection with 15 case studies of small Italian enterprises from the research Sistema Design Italia.

# Chapter 7

## *BROADENING HUMAN POSSIBILITIES THROUGH DESIGN*

The design of wheelchairs offers a unique opportunity to apply what we have discussed thus far about design-inspired innovation, meaning in products, and how a design system functions.

Throughout the world, people with mobility impairments need wheelchairs for their daily physical and social lives. (Impairment is any temporary or permanent loss or abnormality of a body structure or function.) Changing values and more open views on diversity and inclusiveness in society have helped grow interest in and increase efforts toward better wheelchair design, while new material technology, such as lightweight materials and sophisticated electronics, have helped enable it even further. In the last 10 years, innovation in both the powered and non-powered wheelchair segments has increased and progressed to the point that disabled people have many options, including wheelchairs with better interfaces such as joysticks, intelligent controls that use embedded microprocessors, and products that allow them to participate in a wide array of sports and even, most recently, to climb stairs. Through the prism of design-inspired innovation, here we examine the role of lead users in the development of these improved products as well as the influence of industrial design and new technologies.

Today, there are more than 100 million people worldwide with significant mobility impairments. Rory Cooper, a lead wheelchair user active in design and development, estimates that they represent nearly $1 trillion in global buying power, and mobility devices exceed $1 billion in annual revenues.[1] The Swedish Federation for the Disabled estimates that in Sweden some 8 percent of the population has impairments that affect mobility, and of these about 100,000 people need wheelchairs for their daily life. In addition, each year about half a million people worldwide get spinal cord injuries (added to the more than 100 million people with similar injuries). Most of these people — around 55 percent — use their wheelchairs all of the time.[2]

In keeping with our discussion in the preceding chapter, a wheelchair should be regarded not only as a physical object but also as a product with an implicit message. The product not only signifies its basic functions — and aesthetics — but also carries an emotional and symbolic value with a set of symbolic meanings for both the user and individuals observing its use. In this respect, it is an ideal example of how a design-inspired innovation *creates* meaning.

## The wheelchair as an extension of body and mind

Throughout history, the progress of wheelchair development has been ploddingly slow. Most of the products currently in use were developed in the last 20 years, and many people still use traditional hospital devices, which are not amenable to an active life.[3] Despite the tremendous need for active wheelchairs in developing countries, their availability is quite limited. In Africa, for instance, there is a very low interest in developing and marketing state-of-the-art wheelchairs because the basic view accorded of disabilities differs widely from the view developed in many of the industrialized countries over the past two decades. Of course it is also a matter of available resources in medical care and the society as a whole.

The challenge for a modern society is to increase opportunities for people with disabilities to maximize their potential and quality of life. This requires better rehabilitation engineering and innovation, design, and product development that will help disabled individuals lead active and productive lives. Increasingly, mobility-impaired people are demanding new technologies that will help them maintain an active lifestyle as they grow older. Today, an estimated 5 percent of people over age 70 are wheelchair users.[4] Yet, the design of many wheelchairs has not changed fundamentally since wheelchairs were first introduced.

### Sports for People with Mobility Impairments

Mobility impairments are no longer an impediment to people's participation in sports. Sweden, for instance, has established 18 different sports since 1969 as part of the Swedish Sports Federation for Disabled (SHIF), which has 35,000 active members. These include wheelchair basketball, rugby, track and field, table tennis, sledge hockey, and dancing. About 30–40 percent of SHIF members have mobility impairments and are active in different wheelchair sports.

The Development Center for Disability Sports in Eskilstuna, Sweden conducts several ongoing research and development projects through which it cooperates with researchers and students at Mälardalen University, SHIF, and lead users in sports and the design of wheelchairs. In one project, "Multisport Wheel Chair," Mälardalen engineering students designed and constructed various models for flexible wheelchairs (Exhibit 7.1 presents some of the models). The aim is to make it easier for people to start and test various sports activities.

Exhibitions of the output of these projects have taken place as part of "The Swedish Design Year 2005" in Sweden and Greece and at the Paralympic Winter Games in Turin, Italy in March 2006.

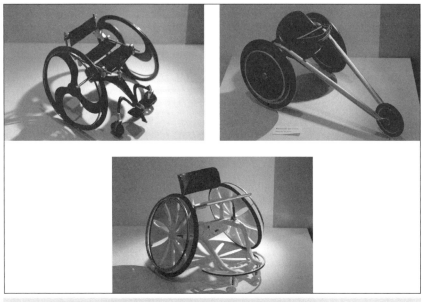

**Exhibit 7.1.** Examples of multi-sport wheelchairs (models in 1:3 Scale).

A common issue faced by the wheelchair user is how his own identity changes, both in his own as well as in others' perceptions.[5] A wheelchair allows a person with disabilities to be more independent and take greater control over his or her life, especially if the chair is well designed and is user-friendly. The product acts as a physical extension of the human body and mind by giving the user independence and identity.

**Lead users as innovators**

The development of wheelchairs for active use and sports involves close ties between lead users and manufacturers. Some leading manufacturers have even emerged under the management of successful wheelchair sportsmen who are both designers and innovators, and among whom a global network community of competence has developed.

As von Hippel writes; "User innovation networks may, but need not, incorporate the qualities of user communities, where these are defined as ... networks of interpersonal ties that provide sociability, support, information, a sense of belonging and social identity. Sports groups [offered] the qualities of communities to participants."[6] For example, wheelchairjunkie.com gets more than 125,000 hits per month and is one of the most active wheelchair discussion websites. The webmaster, Mark Smith, became so well known that Pride Mobility hired him as a manager and designer.

Manual wheelchairs with design improvements focus mainly around creating lightweight designs with new materials (aluminum, titanium, carbon fiber), alternative frame configurations, suspension systems, ergonomics, adjustable features, wheel improvements, and aesthetics. The trend in wheelchairs for active use and sports is to use titanium material in the frame and carbon fiber material in the wheels, which results in very light — but expensive — wheelchairs. According to Jalle Jungnell, owner of Panthera, a leading Swedish manufacturer, wheelchairs today weigh less than half of what they weighed in 1976. The stainless wheelchair was used at the 1976 Paralympics in Toronto. At the end of the 1970s, aluminum wheel frames were introduced, followed in the mid-1980s by the first titanium frame. In 1990, carbon fiber materials were introduced in the wheels.

Research[7] indicates that ultra-light chairs tend to increase mobility and reduce the risk of secondary injury. Additionally, studies suggest that proper chair setup and training may reduce the risk for developing injury. Other important findings included moving the rear-wheel axles closer to the wheelchair's centre of mass and applying smooth, fluid strokes.

Design is important in many aspects. Bo Lindkvist, a former world-class wheelchair marathoner and product manager at ETAC — a leading wheelchair manufacturer — explains that it is design that allows for new perspectives from the start and throughout the entire process. "Industrial designers have a holistic, more ergonomic, aesthetic, and user friendly view. We would never have been so successful without industrial designers. It is impossible to run and succeed in bringing a project to market without an industrial designer on the project team." Lindkvist's vision for the future of active wheelchair design and development comprises more tailor-made wheelchairs, ordered online by users from the district center, to the company; simplicity in all aspects (manufacturing, user adjustment, easy handling, etc.); innovations in the suspension system (no more inflatable tires); and a product development process that always begins with design and marketing, not technology.

Bob Hall, another wheelchair innovator and designer, lives in Cambridge, Massachusetts. He began designing wheelchairs in his mother's basement in the mid-1970s and founded his company, New Halls Wheels, in 1984. In 1974, he became the first person to compete in the Boston Marathon in a wheelchair, which opened the door for many future road racers. That same year, he also won the world's first wheelchair marathon, held in Ohio. Exhibit 7.2 shows one of his designs for a modern racing wheelchair.

Like Hall, other lead users in wheelchair design and innovation have contributed to many development aspects. They have acted as role

**Exhibit 7.2.** A modern racing wheelchair.

models and opened doors for active wheelchair users, including showing how wheelchair design is "good business with meaning" and can improve the quality of life.

In the last 10 years, several new types of wheelchairs have been developed and introduced to the market. Hand-cycle wheelchairs for active use and sports are designed with lightweight materials and good ergonomics. The marketplace also includes wheelchairs with outstanding features, and powered wheelchairs with scooter technology and better interfaces such as joysticks and intelligent controls (thanks to embedded microprocessors). One innovative wheelchair (discussed in greater detail below) can even go over rough terrain and balance on two wheels for climbing stairs.

Rory Cooper has dedicated his life and professional work to better wheelchair design. After being hit by a bus and speeding truck, he nearly died. His first wheelchair weighed 80 pounds (36.3 kg) and was made of steel. From the moment he left the hospital, he says, he hated that chair. Ever since, he has been building wheelchairs and making important research contributions in the field of wheel-chair selection, testing, and configuration. Cooper, a bronze medalist in the 1988 Paralympic Games, is now recognized as one of the world's foremost authorities in wheelchair design and technology and is a professor at the University of Pittsburgh's Human Engineering Research Laboratories (HERL). His ideal is that the wheelchair must be thought of as an *extension of self* and as *a means of self-expression*. But some of the wheelchairs in use today, he says, are outdated and even dangerous, and just do not make the cut. They are poorly designed products that can likely lead to other, secondary disabilities.

What do people such as Hall, Lindkvist, Jungnell, Tommy Olsson (inventor and product developer at Invacare), and Cooper have in common? All five have mobility impairments and are active wheelchair users. Furthermore, they have been successful as world-class athletes and have competed with each other or are participants in the same network of lead users. And they are broadening human possibilities through their designs, which speak a language of *mobility*.

**An innovative mobility device**

One of the most innovative wheelchairs ever developed is the Independence 3000 iBOT™, a revolutionary mobility device for the disabled developed by DEKA (Exhibit 7.3). Johnson & Johnson introduced it to the market in 2004.[8] In 2005, Johnson & Johnson announced market introduction of its next generation developed by Independence Technology (a J&J Company). Rory Cooper and his HERL research team tested it and concluded that it "is a functional mobility device that expands the options of wheelchair users. It is most useful outdoors and where there is sufficient space to use its unique *balance* function."[9]

DEKA, a research and development firm in the United States, was founded in 1982 by Dean Kamen, an award-winning inventor and

**Exhibit 7.3.** The Independence iBOT™.

entrepreneur who holds more than 150 patents worldwide, many of them for innovative medical devices. In the 1980s, he invented the first wearable infusion pump and, after forming the company, went on to develop a climate system control and a new helicopter design. He also introduced a more general device, the Segway Human Transporter, based on the balancing technology that had its first application in the iBOT™. The company, which focuses on developing breakthrough medical devices that change people's lives, employs some 200 people, mostly engineers, and often pursues new technologies in search of new applications.

The company fosters innovation and encourages questioning and unconventional thinking. J. Douglas Field, who was the technical leader for the iBOT™ from 1997 to 1999 in his capacity as vice president for product development, explains that Kamen is always on the lookout for important problems. The idea for working on mobility for people with disabilities came to Kamen one day when he saw a young man in a wheelchair struggling to get over a curb. An intense person with deep concern for the welfare of others, he obsessed about the unfairness of the situation and how the world is architected for people who can walk.[10]

Kamen, according to Field, is said to have many invention principles "hardwired" in his head and is obsessed with compressed air, the ferromagnetic effect, and nitinol. He eschews incremental innovation, focusing instead on difficult problems he believes the company can help solve. At his company, he has created an environment that produces a disproportionate number of breakthrough products. He inspires his staff of engineers to work on the development and commercial execution of many new-to-the-world products. To demonstrate the non-linear way in which innovation often occurs for breakthrough products, consider the tongue-in-cheek diagram in Exhibit 7.4. The exhibit shows the creativity, intensity, and drive of this entrepreneur/ inventor.[11]

Discovering that balance is something that makes humans unique was the breakthrough for Kamen's work. It allowed him to think about the mobility problem in a different way. Although Kamen was not the first person to use gyroscopes for balance and mobility, his company was the first to apply this concept successfully to wheelchair design. Kamen explained the significance of his insight for mobility and the importance of balance: "Your mother remembers your first steps. It is a big deal

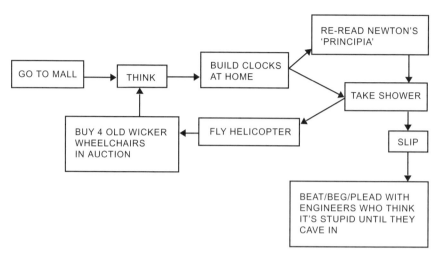

**Exhibit 7.4.** The type of creativity process that results in an iBOT™.

that humans walk around. It is difficult to do. Balance is fundamental to the way we get around."[12]

Solving the balance problem was key to solving everything else. The result was a self-balancing mobility machine that enables users to climb stairs, and negotiate sand, rocks, and curbs. This machine can stand up and balance the way humans do. The mobility system balances and rises on two wheels to get to high shelves in the kitchen or the supermarket. Restoring balance to disabled people also achieved something even more dramatic and unintended — it elevated disabled people so they could see at ordinary eye level instead of looking at others' waists. Being able to meet people at eye level turns out to have a significant, if unintended, psychological benefit and something that no other mobility device for the disabled had accomplished before. Tammy Wilbur, a 24-year-old paraplegic who tested the product, best expressed the significance of this achievement: "I haven't felt like this in a long time — tall. It is difficult always being short."[13]

The mobility device changed the *language*. It provides ". . . experiences which have no price, with parameters that can't be measured by engineers."[14] Even if they were unable to anticipate these messages beforehand, engineers who come to understand the benefits of the product once it is in the hands of the user can still *feel* these parameters.

DEKA exhibits a productive marriage of innovation cultures. Terence Conran, a famous English designer, says it can be difficult to draw the line between design, invention, and technological innovation. In his view, the inventor and the designer are rarely the same person. The process of turning an invention into an innovation demands other skill sets.[15] For this reason, invention, innovation, and design need each other, as close yet distinct partners in the creative thinking process.

One of the key challenges in new product development is the fundamental contradiction between the culture and people good at ideation, and those executing the design. Nowhere is this contradiction more intense than in the development of applications new to the world that require creative thinking and precision engineering. A unique aspect of the company culture is that, as an organization, it is able to tolerate the diversity required to be good at both ideation and execution. Of course, it helps that one of the key ideation people is the company president but, to his credit, Kamen recognizes that he needs engineers who are experts at execution to develop his new products. Field observes that there are important differences between "ideation-focused" and "execution-focused" cultures, and there is a need to marry the two diverse cultures to develop innovative products. "The best ideation people will never really appreciate the work it takes to bring a product to commercialization." By the same token, he says, "the best execution people will never figure out what it is that ideation people do with their day. Get them to work together and you will change the world."[16]

### The making of meaning and meaningful products

What is the real meaning of things surrounding us and what symbols do these things represent? Psychologists Mihaly Csikszentmihalyi and Eugene Rochberg-Halton have reflected on the personification of things rather than the reification of persons: "Things embody goals, make skills manifest, and shape the identity of their users. His self is to a large extent a reflection of things with which he interacts. Thus objects also make and use their makers and users."[17] They view a "thing" as any unit of information that has recognizable identity in consciousness and call it a "sign." From this perspective, a symbol is only one kind of sign, defined as the representation of some object, quality, physical thing, or idea.

One could say that meaning is a process of communication involving signs and symbols. However relative to other signs — such as emotions or ideas — objects possess concreteness and are grounded in their physical structure. An artifact from an ancient people can still convey an image of the ideas of that culture even though there may be no record of how those people spoke or what they believed. When a thing *means* something to someone, it is interpreted in the context of past experiences, either consciously, or unconsciously in the form of habit. To restrict the perspective even further, objects are shaped by human intentionality and human-made things are dependent on intention to exist. This is part of the language that a design can create and shape.

Things people use, own, and surround themselves with can also reflect aspects of the owner's personality. For example, clothes, cars, furnishings, art, and books could all be expressions of one's self. Additionally, our things are signs and part of the process that constitutes consciousness in a person.[18] Here we can find similarities between the psychologists Csikszentmihalyi and Rochberg-Halton and the user/ designer/scientist Rory Cooper's view of the wheelchair as an extension of self, and also as a means of self-expression. From a psychosocial perspective, a wheelchair is much like a person's clothing — a shoe or a glove — and style is an important aspect of any design.

Dan Buchner of Design Continuum suggests that successful product design must strike a balance between capturing the hearts of consumers and achieving the financial returns desired by the producer. Designers convey *messages* to consumers through design.[19] They manipulate form, gesture, materials, texture, interaction, and other design elements to convey a message to the consumer, whether consciously or unconsciously. He offers the dictionary definition of *meaning* as "something that is conveyed

**Jenny Lundblad**

In an October 2003 interview with one of the present authors, Jenny Lundblad (featured in Exhibit 7.5) — among the world's best female track and field athletes in wheelchair racing (she competes in the 400 m, 800 m and marathon events) — expressed her feelings about sports, "flow," the quality of life, and also about design.

**Exhibit 7.5.** Jenny Lundblad in competition.

"Sports has given me the joy of life back again," she explains. "I am stronger now in many ways and more independent in my daily life thanks to my sport."

How does Jenny view design? "The wheels are my legs," she says, "and therefore the design is extremely important for me."

or signified, sense or significance." However, he says, meaning is brought to a design not by the designer but by the consumer, and 80 percent of the meaning of a design is in the viewer's *mind*, not in the object. That is why the designer must understand the 80 percent of meaning that lies in the consumer's mind, including the consumer's passions.

Buchner offers a simple example of product meaning in a viewer's mind. An egg from a free-range hen is not the same as an egg from a hen in a small cage. While some aspects of the egg may be the same, consumers perceive the former as healthier. In Denmark, eggs from free-range hens have captured more than 50 percent of the market, despite increased labor and space requirements which raise their cost by some 20 percent.

Victor Papanek is another highly distinguished designer. His book *Design for the Real World* is one of the world's most widely read books on the subject. Papanek's basic view is that "design is the conscious and intuitive effort to impose meaningful order."[20] In other words, a consciousness of thinking, research, and analysis is present in the design process. He also sees design as having a sensing/feeling part, which is not easily articulated in terms of market needs or well-defined problem solving, but more as tacit knowledge and pre-consciousness. The intuitive part focuses on social, ethical, and environmental effects on design of new products, what is actually good and meaningful in a society, and what eases or improves the quality of everyday life.

Signs, symbols, and objects can be seen as expressions of self for status, social integration (or belonging), and social security. On the other hand, one can see them as expressions of differentiation that stress the unique qualities of the owner, and his or her skills and superiority over others. A point made by Cooper illustrates this: "The wheelchair has, for most of its history, been a design that segregated instead of integrated people."[21]

But if an artifact can extend the human body or mind, then what is a person? From a psychological point of view, a person is a subject and has a self with self-awareness and self-control. Self-awareness and self-knowledge occur when the self becomes the object of reflection — that is, the self takes itself as its own object. But self-knowledge is inferential and mediated by signs that comprise language and thought, and is always open to change and development.[22] Objects affect what a person can do, either by expanding or restricting the scope of that person's actions and thoughts. Because what a person does largely represents what he or she is, objects have a determining effect on the development of the self. Therefore, understanding the type of relationship that exists between people and things is crucial to the designer.[23]

The *meaning* in products is a link between our social life and symbols in the product, says Verganti. Meaning not only signifies a product's basic functions and aesthetics, but also carries an emotional and symbolic value, bringing a message — a product message — and a meaning to the user (close to Csikszentmihalyi and Rochberg-Halton's view). As Verganti explains: "Apart from styling, what matters to the user, in addition to the functionality of a product, is its emotional and symbolic value, that is, its meaning."[24]

Similarly, Gotzsch[25] uses product messages and meanings to talk about "meaningful products" and "product charisma." Durgee and Veryzer view the object of marketing as giving a personality or soul to a tangible product so that it comes alive.[26] They also use the emotional term "product soul" — inspired by Thomas Moore, who regards meaning as a soul in people, in the tree in front of your house, or in your car parked under that tree. Whether natural or human-made, the idea is that this "soul" affects each individual thing.[27]

Danish designer Per Mollerup views human needs in a hierarchic way and looks at design, similarly, as having three levels. According to Mollerup, as soon as man's most elementary demands are satisfied to ensure survival, other demands arise. Simultaneously, it appears that the original demands can be satisfied in a more sophisticated way than was first assumed, which makes life easier. Gradually, as acute needs can be met and dangers averted, the desire to make life more comfortable is manifested and man finds he can afford to have feelings. His demands take on an emotional context and life becomes more interesting.[28]

The psychologist Abraham Maslow's hierarchy of needs is close to this view. Consider a combination of the different phases in his hierarchy with the tasks of product design. A practical product fulfills *basic needs*, but its use can also improve *safety and comfort*. When that product creates affection between the user and the product, it satisfies needs for *love and belonging*. By communicating the social position of its user, the product satisfies *status and self-esteem* needs. Finally — and here is where the design-inspired wheelchair innovations come in — the product creates the possibility for *self-actualization* by addressing meaning and the quality of life. From Maslow's point of view it would be possible to expand the term "meaning" and "meaningful" to meaningful products and meaningful work.

Krippendorff also discusses meaning in products and relates it to product semantics: "Meaning is a cognitively constructed relationship. It selectively connects features of an object and features of its (real environment or imagined) context into a coherent unity." In other words, objects must always be seen in a context and the product environment of other things, situations, and users, including the observer himself.

If we want to define what a meaningful product could be, we must first examine what is meant by self-actualization. To use Maslow's metaphor, it is like being on an ocean of waves, a series of highs and lows. To achieve the highest level, one needs the opportunity to use and expand his or her individual and human resources. Of course, everyone is different and has varying levels of need at each level, but, according to Maslow, all levels must be personally satisfied to get to "the top." *In many situations, we need to design and use products to satisfy our needs.* As Mollerup says, the hammer, cup, and wheels serve as extensions for us to get our needs satisfied and to reach our goals. Today modern information and communication technology such as computers, mobile telephones, and CD players also serve as such extensions when they expand our senses in time and place.

Our needs are not static. They are dynamic and demanding in the ways in which individuals will always reach higher for more and better situations. Drucker has pointed out, from an innovation perspective,[29] that innovations and development begin with a conscious search for opportunities. The sources of innovation can be found in several different opportunities, one of which is change in perception. He views the phenomenon using the old metaphor of a glass being half-empty or half-full, but with vastly different meanings. A change in perception from half-full to half-empty opens up big innovation opportunities. Such changes do not alter facts, but can dramatically change their meaning. As an example, Drucker looks at the state of America's health — it has never been better, he says, yet people are not satisfied. Demands will increase according to the opportunities in the given and present society.

### Broadening possibilities through design

One challenge for a modern society is to increase the opportunity *for all people* to maximize their potential and quality of life. A large number of aging people, particularly in developed countries, have the expectation that they will be able to continue to live an active life despite their advancing age. Increasingly, they are demanding new technologies that will help them maintain an active lifestyle. We saw in Chapter 4 how the MIT AgeLab is addressing these issues from a comprehensive design point of view.

For people with impaired mobility, a wheelchair is both a physical object and a product with an implicit message. It not only signifies its basic functions — and aesthetics — but also carries an emotional and symbolic value with a set of symbolic meanings for both the user and individuals observing its use. In the eyes of users, designers of wheelchairs have created *language*.

Lead users have taken a leadership role in developing this language and spurring design — or, in many cases — designing wheelchairs themselves. Design is driving, indeed, *inspiring*, innovation.

What does the future hold? Will the degree to which innovation is inspired by design grow? How does a designer innovate? These questions are addressed in our final chapter.

## Endnotes

[1]R.A. Cooper, 2001, p. v.

[2]R.A. Cooper, 1998.

[3]Cooper 1998, p. 2.

[4]U. Sonn and G. Grimby, 1994, p. 10.

[5]Cooper, 1998, pp. 1 and 10–11.

[6]Cooper, 1998. See also von Hippel, 2002, p. 27, quoted from Franke and Shah, 2002, How Communities Support Innovative Activities: An Exploration of Assistance and Sharing Among End-users. MIT Sloan School, working paper. In *Democratizing Innovation* (2005), von Hippel develops his thoughts and findings further about user-centered innovation and communities of lead-users in innovation processes in different fields, for example, in sports, surgical equipment and software.

[7]R.A. Cooper, R. Cooper, and M.L. Boninger, *Sports 'n Spokes Magazine*, March 2002 (www.sportsnspokes.com) (an article about a lightweight survey of 20 years' development).

[8]E.I. Schwartz, 2002. Also www.dekareserach.com (2003) and www.independencenow. com/Ibot (2003).

[9]R.A. Cooper *et al.*, 2003.

[10]J. Douglas Field, presentation to students at Rensselaer Polytechnic Institute, Troy, NY, 2001.

[11]*Ibid*.

[12]D. Kamen, statement on ABC News' Nightline, May 1999.

[13]T. Wilbur, statement on ABC News' Nightline, May 1999.

[14]J. Hockenberry, statement on ABC News' Nightline, May 1999.

[15]T. Conran, 1996.

[16]J. Douglas Field, *op cit*.

[17]M. Csikszentmihalyi and E. Rochberg-Halton, 1981. p. 1.

[18]Csikszentmihalyi and Rochberg-Halton, 1981.

[19]D. Buchner, 2003.

[20]V. Papanek, 1985, p. 4. (Reprinted 2004).

[21]Cooper, 1998, p. 1.

[22]Cooper, 1998, p. 2–3.

[23]Cooper, 1998, pp. 10–11 and 53.

[24]R. Verganti 2003.

[25]J. Gotzsch, 2000; Gotzsch, 2002.

[26]J. Durgee and R.W. Veryzer, 1999, p. 6.

[27]T. Moore, 1992, p. 268.

[28]P. Mollerup, 1986, p. 20.

[29]P.F. Drucker, 1985, p. 6.

# Chapter 8

## *DESIGN — VISION AND VISUALIZING*

Why has design-driven innovation emerged now as a crucial issue and driving force? What does it offer us? What might the future hold? Might design-inspired innovation be nothing more than a fad? Is there merit to our contention that delighting the customer, emphasizing simplicity and elegance, and creating meaning are the essence of success?

### Why design now?

Not everything that seems to be a fad *is* a fad. They often become standard arrows in the management quiver. Several reasons may be suggested for why industrial design has become "hot." One is the rise in complexity. To take a somewhat extreme but illustrative example, life emerged out of a primal soup of, say, six essential elements. In a bootstrapping process, reliant upon catalysis and autocatalysis and competition and selection, ever more complex structures arose.[1] Likewise, newer technology is created with the assistance of new technology in an ever-ascending march forward.

In one example from design, certain geometrical forms found in the latest cars were made possible only with the assistance of the most recent version of CAD software. Complexity also arises from a process of recombination: micromechanical systems benefit from advances in semiconductor electronics; optical fibers substitute for electric wiring in cars; and so on. Industrial designers, as brokers of knowledge and spanners of boundaries, may themselves contribute to this increase in complexity.

It is a generally accepted axiom that complexity is associated with some cost. American composer Harry Partch wrote music that employs 42 notes to the octave, and this requires novel instruments and profoundly re-trained musical performers.[2] We might associate with dictionary-style users' manuals, on paper or as interfaces designed for accessing functions.

To the end user, complexity is not necessarily a virtue. The end user does not celebrate the complexity of what is "inside" a product, system, or service. Increasingly, it falls upon the designer to simplify and concentrate, to distil the essentials, to make that complexity invisible — as in the iPod.

Design matters also because of what might be called technology's "vanishing act," embodied in a concept such as nano-technology. This, too, is related to the increase in complexity. Nanotech connotes something small, be it found in the realm of mechanics, biology, or electronics — so small as to be invisible without a microscope (or a nanoscope which logically would be the next instrument to zoom in on the incredibly small). Technology is, of course, "vanishing" also in the sense that as it more and more concerns software, services, and experiences — the end user does not see the technology in the forms of hardware. Again, the end user is little concerned with the insides, or with technology at all, but much more concerned with function, reliability, ease of use, safety, and so on. Increasingly, the designer is called upon to re-design real products to become "virtual."

Mensch claimed that when technologies mature, the characteristics of products converge and styling or "cosmetics" provide the distinguishing factors;[3] the same might be said to hold for commodities in general. (The Chiquita brand provides an example of the designing and branding of a true commodity: the banana.) An average grocery store stocks nearly 50,000 different products, a threefold increase in 20 years. A look into a more specialized store, such as one for consumer electronics, provides a similar display of product proliferation: one calculation holds that an average of more than 6 million different systems configurations are offered. TNS Media Intelligence has two million brands in its database, and adds another 700 each day. In 2003 alone, 26,893 new food and household products were introduced, including 115 deodorants, 187 breakfast cereals, and 303 women's fragrances, according to Mintel International Group Ltd.'s Global New Products Database. And products reach markets faster: the PC took seven years to reach 1 million users, while the first-generation Sony PlayStation took 10 months. Its successor took all of two days.

Researchers have also noted an explosion in studies geared at mapping customization, reflecting a trend of precisely that: customization. Today's technology is very far from Taylor's "one best solution" or Ford's "any color as long as it's black." It allows for tailoring to specific needs, at almost no cost except for the time required for organizing. More than

10 years ago, Panasonic offered its Japanese buyers a choice between some 11 million different bicycles at affordable prices and produced them in just two days. To guard the image of exclusive, individually assembled products, delivery times were set much longer. As an ultimate step to customization, companies in certain product or service categories have started engaging customers in designing their own individual products.

**Visual versus verbal**

A design must create an emotional response and tell a story. Why? So many new products appear and disappear. So many are little more than variations on a theme. A product and its product family must stand out. It needs to have a strong, coherent, all-comprehending identity. And identity is not just for the product or service, but also for the customer and user. Product type as well as the particular make chosen tells a story about the owner. The Miata and Harley-Davidson clubs did not form by chance.

Design is both a noun and a verb. As a noun, design is what the user perceives; as a verb it is the process by which the designer produces that perception. The noun is the visual embodiment; the verb, to a large extent, relies upon visualization and modeling. Visualization should be taken in a broader sense than just creating something we see; sounds and tactile sensations are also part of designing for a particular identity. Much of design, in this sense, is about synthesis and integration.

The left–right brain duality has long been thought to encompass something broader than a division of language functions and visual-spatial reasoning. Researchers make a distinction between processing what is new and what is not: "[T]he right hemisphere is the novelty hemisphere, the daring hemisphere, the explorer of the unknown and the uncharted."[4] Brain-imaging studies show the right hemisphere, the one engaged in visual thinking, is activated when we are in the early stages of acquiring a new cognitive skill.

Psychologist Jonathan W. Schooler has found another effect, also of relevance to our discussion, which he calls verbal overshadowing. It implies that as long as we remember something visually — a face, for example — we have no difficulty in picking it out in a crowd or from a photograph. But if we were triggered to describe the face in words, that visual memory is displaced as thinking moves from the right to the left hemisphere. For many things — certainly for faces — we are much better at visual recognition than at verbal description. For insight problems requiring a flash of discovery, Schooler demonstrated that people who were asked to detail their thinking process solved 30 percent fewer problems.[5] However, for logic problems, problem solving is not impaired.

Gedenryd suggests that it is entirely artificial and counter-productive to see a boundary between the problem solver and the world in which the problem exists (he goes on to make the same claim for the boundary normally seen as existing between the cognizant individual and the world around him or her). Interaction is needed with — and within — the world of the problem, rather than demanding a set problem specification.[6] Like Gedenryd, Schön takes architects and designers as his main example when opposing Simon's claim that it should be possible to create an heuristic algorithm for "general problem solving" — even for "messy" or ill-defined problems.[7] Schön demonstrates how designers work on reformulating the tasks, and also how they are influenced by experience and tacit knowledge.[8]

**Numbers versus stories**

Numbers and written words characterize such specifications, as they do contracts and orders for undertakings within and between organizations. Though they are often useful, as when they prompt observation and the collection of data, they may be dangerous. Beyond verbal overshadowing, they may cause us to constrain our perception, particularly to the extent that they count only on quantitative data and tangible facts, static freeze-frames of dynamic processes. Here again, an interactive approach might be needed. Petroski, for one, holds up examples from the history of technology where numbers and written words substituted for drawings, making it practically impossible to obtain an overview that gives a sense of the whole system, and thus resulting in rather dire consequences.[9] One of his examples is the Tacoma Narrows Bridge catastrophe, with his conclusion: "Because the new breed of engineers believed that they were calculating, with the deflection theory, the stresses and strains more accurately than nineteenth-century engineers like Telford and Roebling, their classic works were conveniently taken as aesthetic rather than structural models."[10] Swift describes the development of a matrix that allows customers to choose the features of a scanner handle, including comfort, perception, and efficiency, through human factors analysis.[11]

### Communicating through sketching

Designers have a particular facility for sketching (see Appendix B). Their brainstorming activities may entirely forego verbally formulated ideas, with sketches circulated or adorning the session room walls instead. Sketching is a practice that, in itself, functions as a creativity stimulating process and helps designers get into the head of the end user, possibly evoking his or her creativity, since it serves as an efficient communication tool (again avoiding verbal overshadowing). Rapidly made sketches may give the potential end user a concrete image of the future solution that words alone could never convey. Alternatives may also be easily presented.

A few designers rely entirely upon computer-aided design software, but most prefer to sketch by hand in the earliest stages. In the words of Swedish design star Hans Erich: "Computers aren't tactile." As Schenk said: "Your hand is part of your brain. It's as though your brain is drawing."[12] Sketching by hand allows a designer to capture an idea quickly; it concentrates on the essentials rather than on bells and whistles. A hand sketch is inexact and its crudeness serves as an invitation to creativity — it provokes new ideas and insights. But it is the speed and facility that Lorenz underlines. "Most engineers find it difficult to sketch," he writes, but it can greatly improve their "ability to help shorten the product development cycle ... by accomplishing through a few quickly done sketches what would take an engineering draughtsman weeks to do, even with the help of CADCAM."[13]

Producing more or less primitive models, mockups, or prototypes, perhaps with rapid prototyping machinery, could also be regarded as sketching in a more general way (it certainly is a form of visualization). The computer-based methods can provide three-dimensional renderings, rotating or moving the "sketch" in realistic ways on the screen and allowing a product to be assembled and disassembled in a virtual world. Thus, end users may observe and react to amazingly realistic representations of products still in the idea stage. There are instances when computerized sketches and mockups presented in brochures and expositions have resulted in order books overflowing for products not yet in existence. And there are other instances when such renderings of yet non-existent — but convincingly designed — products have enticed venture capitalists to open their wallets.

One might see sketches of potential future products or user situations as scenarios that offer a more complete user environment. These dynamic representations give a concomitant feeling of completeness and suggest how the product or service might operate in conjunction with other devices or services. As with sketches, scenarios are tools for communication, allowing for discussions of and reactions to a product only envisaged (and, of course, scenarios constitute a kind of compiled sketches). "Drawing is the key to relating all the elements together."[14]

In the scanner project mentioned earlier, the design team created hundreds of sketches and, through brainstorming, eventually produced more than 150 foam models, "representing a wide range of form and feature explorations."[15] The many alternative sketches demanded early in the development of a new car — typically, 15 or 20 — may allow for the discovery and exploration of different scenarios as well as of different design languages or language expressions. Sketches, whether by hand or computer or carved out of plastic foam, may be situated in user environments and related to customer segments. One of many ways to do this is by envisaging "synthetic customer personalities," or personae, that are seen and described as real. In a way, they are personified user scenarios, useful beyond the design context.

If a sketch in whatever form gives the end user an idea about functionality, it may also offer more than a hint of the design language to be applied. Several such sketches may offer more about what kind of "soul" the product will have than any well-phrased verbal description: emotions, messages, and meanings are tacit, not fully describable with words, formulae, or mathematics.

Sketching offers ways to convey and receive messages about that which is tacit. This is of major importance. Without it, the user may not be able to express his demands or know what he actually prefers. Because they deal in words, market studies and polls mostly leave out questions about tacit issues. In contrast, focus groups conducted by individuals with keen eyes and ears for vague, transient psychological signals may well give some clues in this respect by picking up subtle signals of tacit feelings. One might say that sketches offer an interface between the tacit and the verbally expressed.

**Provocation**

Sketches are productively provocative for several reasons. Architect/ designer Olle Andersson notes one that is perhaps not very obvious: "We often experience that hand and brain are not fully coordinated ... the arm and hand ... don't always obey the brain. A common result is that unwanted lines and fragments of pictures appear on the sketchpad. A line will not be straight, or a curve will be different from ... intended. These unexpected new marks which also can be caused by the drawing material itself can be called random or sometimes scribble. The great thing is that this random picture provides new information; new questions and possibilities continue to arise from it. This phenomenon becomes an important part of the creative process."[16]

Andersson also highlights the important fact that sketches concentrate on the few key features: "Sketches ... depict the real or imagined in a bare, simple way. Only that which at that special moment is essential is allowed to appear in these naive drawings."[17] McKim adds that sketches can be produced quickly and very cheaply, offering many prototypes: "Visual thinkers ... *draw quickly* ... The quickly executed, formative processes of graphic ideation are favored by sketching ... concerned more with chief features than with detail ... *Graphic ideation is visually talking to oneself* ... you can feel free to fail many times on the way to obtaining a solution" (emphases in original).[18]

As with sketches, imperfections in mockups, prototypes, or physical renderings in general may be a boon, contends Schrage: "The strength of rough prototyping media is that they encourage playing with ideas, possibilities, and potential. Roughness encourages questions."[19] Over-prescriptive drawings actually tend to pre-empt creative contributions.[20] Often prototypes also help overcome a fundamental perceptual barrier: "Too many organizations believe that manageability means predictability,"[21] which is concomitant to planning.

As we noted earlier, it is important to see the problem freshly, possibly in a new framework, context, or thought style. Artists and art critics use the old adage that drawing, most of all, stimulates seeing. Thus, McKim concludes, in a work on design activities, it "is an inducement to stop labeling and to look."[22]

But sketching is more than seeing, explains Tom Kelley of IDEO: "Prototyping doesn't just solve straightforward problems. Call it serendipity or even luck, but once you start drawing or making things, you open up new possibilities of discovery ... Doodling, drawing, modeling. Sketch ideas and make things, and you're likely to encourage accidental, discoveries."[23]

The old quandary of whether form follows function — or perhaps today it is other way around — is one that leads back to the traditional design idea of *styling*. Cars, consumer electronics, computers, and telephones are among the growing number of reminders that signify the importance of interaction design. In addition, design may be interpreted as conveying not just function or ease of use but also emotion and meaning. We have already mentioned a product's "soul"; designers try to imbue a product with "a soul" and a narrative, and they try to turn services into "experiences." It would mean damnation for a product to be deemed "soulless" or for a service to be judged a negative experience.

Passenger cars are prime examples of products designed to make statements that tell stories about their owners. Given that fact, and that the greatest opportunities for affecting the outcome of a product development process exist at the beginning of the process, having the end result available early on, in sketch form, might have a great positive impact. The advent of computer assistance has greatly reduced reliance on the cumbersome production of clay and other physical models, not to mention time and development costs.

In a constant dialog between form and function, the design language implied by overall styling may provide an impetus to innovative features on a more detailed level. If a product conveys certain emotions and meanings, designers must take care to emphasize and not contradict them when it comes to functionality. But this is a two-way street: certain desirable functions may be styled differently or organized in a way designed to make them conform to the overall design language of a product family and message of the product. To reference cars again, that certain design features, messages, and meanings have very long-term repercussions also holds for many other products. Moreover, the car example evokes the importance of styling for entire product families or portfolios.

**Visualization**

Focus might, profitably, be broadened beyond sketching to include other possibilities: prototyping, modeling, and manipulation of physical artifacts. Miller has provided a general, or cross-disciplinary, study of the application of visualization in several fields, from art to science. He suggests: "In summary, the nature of visual perception is still not completely understood ... But among what is known is that it's a massively parallel process …" After reviewing a number of cases of "imagery and creativity in science and art," he concludes that visual imagery plays a causal role in scientific creativity.[24]

In one concrete example from industry, British Petroleum has installed 3D visualization centers in more than a dozen of its locations. These have yielded great gains not only by stimulating discussion of increasingly creative and integrated alternatives for development, but also by eliciting a rich variety of tacit knowledge from participants in the resulting "virtual reality" simulations of proposed developments. The Harvard-MIT Division of Health Sciences and Technology provides an example that is neither exclusively industry nor research. HST's Martinos Center for Biomedical Imaging has brought a new dimension to medical diagnosis through visualization of both the body's structure and function and of changes in both. The developing approaches have the potential to add profound richness and depth to medical diagnosis and treatment, with visualization complementing or superseding mere calculation.

Many media may be required to achieve visualization, depending upon the actors involved, the problem, and a host of other factors. One factor is the sheer power to convince or to communicate accurately and powerfully: "It's easy to reject a dry report or a flat drawing," writes Kelley. "But models often surprise, making it easier to change your mind and accept new ideas. Or make hard choices, such as foregoing costly and complex features … but a prototype is almost like a spokesperson for a particular point of view, crystallizing the group's feedback and keeping things moving … a good prototype is worth [a] thousand pictures."[25]

"Prototype" is a word often associated with the physical world. For more abstract processes and interrelationships, we may resort to more abstract models that are then used for simulations. Within the Shell Oil company, for example, this was done at first with more than a little hesitance: "'We don't play with models in the boardroom', one manager declared. So Schwartz began playing with the model himself. Gradually, the managing directors began to speak up. After an hour, 'they couldn't leave ... They were totally hooked'."[26]

While not produced as rapidly as sketches, prototypes may still equate with gains in development time because they resonate more with end users. "The developers then moved on to rapid development of a prototype," writes Schrage. "The goal was to present the client with a quick-and-dirty prototype within a fortnight. Why? Because it's far easier for clients to articulate what they want by playing with prototypes than by enumerating requirements. People don't order ingredients from a menu; they order meals."[27]

Schrage provides data on the results of different approaches to development, with "prototypers" performing well, although with different qualities from the contrasting approach:

"Boehm had assigned seven teams of software developers to produce versions of the same cost-estimation model. Three used a prototyping approach; the others a spec-driven. All produced roughly the same product with roughly comparable performance. But ... the prototypers' programs used 40 percent less code and expended 45 percent less effort. The prototyped products rated lower in functionality and ability to handle erroneous inputs but significantly higher in ease of learning and use — that is, their customers liked them more … The prototyped software rated far higher in maintainability … conclusions were unambiguous: prototyping produced a smaller product of equivalent performance with less effort … The user interfaces were also rated superior … it's readily apparent that two different design sensibilities led to fundamentally different design behaviors."[28]

We can find good examples of the systematic manipulation of physical artifacts in the history of technology and especially of invention: "Edison's inventions … used old ideas, materials, or objects in new ways," explain Hargadon and Sutton. "The phonograph blended elements from past work on telegraphs, telephones, and electric motors."[29]

**Playing with real objects and analogs**

One consequence of the productivity in ideation based upon "playing with" physical artifacts is the idea of creating a "memory" out of such physical artifacts, materialized in, for example, IDEO's Tech Box: "It's harder to keep ideas alive when they're not embedded in tangible objects … the memories in the Tech Boxes would soon die if the designers didn't constantly look at the stuff, play with it, and use it in their work. Each Tech Box is now maintained by a local curator and each piece is documented on IDEO's intranet."[30]

Schrage goes on to summarize the advantages of "playing with prototypes": "Quickly and continuously converting new ideas into crude mock-ups and working models turns traditional perceptions of the crude innovation cycle inside out: instead of using the innovation process to come up with finished prototypes, the prototypes themselves drive the innovation process."[31] We recall Schön's reflective practitioner looking from the inside and out.

Prototypes help to facilitate communication between the people involved in a development. According to Schrage, prototypes help externalize ideas, create a language, and make people face and solve problems impossible to visualize in the mind. Prototypes bring teams together, providing a material motivation and stimulating the mind to conceive new perspectives and create a shared space for communication. "Prototypes ... externalize thought and spark conversation. They're 'bandwidth-boosters' and context-creators for both information management and human interaction ... They are inherently social media and mechanisms. More often than not, they become the organization's *lingua franca*, or *medium francum*, bridging its multiple Departments of Babel."[32]

Analogy is a time-honored tool for generating new ideas and solving problems. When industrial designers are seen as boundary spanners, analogies may play an additional role: "... analogies allow [knowledge brokers, viz. designers] to move knowledge from one context to another ... Analogic thinking creates new knowledge by removing it from one context and placing it in another."[33]

Metaphor is a potential tool for bridging language and knowledge context gaps; we might reasonably suggest that it be used as well as a tool for sketching and bringing diverse elements together. Holland describes a metaphor as involving a source and a target, both "surrounded by an aura of meaning and associations [and the] metaphor causes a kind of recombination of these auras, enlarging the perceptions associated." He goes on to quote Black: "The metaphor selects, emphasizes, suppresses, and organizes features of the principal subject by implying statements about it that normally apply to the subsidiary subject."[34] Again, to what extent do industrial designers apply metaphor in their work intuitively, consciously, or perhaps even systematically?

Most industrial designers prefer to start with pen and pencil sketches and later move to clay or styrofoam. With the advent of CAD, CAM, and 3D prototyping, we meet new technologies that can further newer designs: think about "faxing" a product. The perfection of CAD may have a dark flipside, however, by focusing early interest and concern on minor details rather than broad principles. What could replace the creativity-inducing slip of the pen?

It is, of course, conceivable that we will see the development of computer tools that allow for inspired doodling and creation of imperfect forms, stimulating new ideas. We will probably get tactile input devices that give the same "feel" for a product's physical form that mechanical machinery gives us now. We may even see computer tools developed that reverse the process of verbal overshadowing.

Computers amplify human faculties in ways that are still being discovered. Harold Cohen is a pioneer in using computers for producing art.[35] While on an excursion to an old, abandoned Native American village, he was stunned by the fact that the art engraved on rocks there featured eye-pleasing forms ("primitives") similar to those he preferred to produce on his computer. There are certainly tasks computers can never do; they may allow for us to experiment and gain better understanding of what is visually pleasing and elegant. (Douglas Hofstadter has done this in designing typefaces.[36]) Or we may discover limitations to what we can understand.

### Deep simplicity?

Technology helps provide functionality, a quality that is now taken for granted. Products, systems, and services are evolving to be agreeable, pleasurable, providing experiences, telling stories, and expressing identity and authenticity. Open standards allow for interaction, compatibility, and integration. They allow for movement within and also between platforms, with modularity providing another kind of openness — that of changing the "geometry" or the interfaces of the design.

The distinctions between the real and the virtual become "imaginary" as products evolve into services and services into vehicles for self-expression and personal development. Design is being employed to bring the end user closer to the very basic ideas behind an offering, communicating and interacting with it as intimately, intuitively, and transparently as with a close friend or family member — with feelings evoked much like those for a fine piece of art.

This integrating in a number of dimensions receives important impetus from industrial designers' facility for brokering and boundary spanning, something conducive to their clustering geographically, possibly making them co-locate with colleagues displaying complementary capabilities. Their contributions to synthesis and the creation of an entity and wholeness are furthered by their competencies in visualization. If designs are to evoke positive emotions, tell interesting stories, and communicate pregnant identities, it is difficult to avoid seeing them as providing something we call "beauty."

The term "technology" has its root in a Greek word, *techne*. Originally, this stood for both function and form: that which functioned well was also beautiful; artisanship was art and function simultaneously. Then they separated: "The tension between creativity and craft runs through the whole modern history of the creative ... arts."[37]

Arnold Schoenberg's 12-tone music provides a rigorous paradigm for the composer and elegant procedures, although hardly anyone could stand to listen to the music produced. Are we perhaps closing the circle, coming back to simple, straightforward beauty as an overarching principle for products and services, and demoting technology to something hidden in and relegated to their deeper recesses?

We believe the evidence shows that we are indeed coming (returning?) to innovation inspired by design that truly delights the user. These are the products that integrate the tangible and the intangible, the physical product and the service — and thus enhance the experience of the customer. In our examples, it is not technology in the driver's seat. Bells and whistles do not rule the day. Rather, it is the enduring qualities of simplicity and elegance.

Indeed, design-inspired innovation is creativity of a higher order.

## Endnotes

[1] R. Kurzweil is among those who has amassed evidence of accelerating complexity. See R. Kurzweil, 2005; see also http://www.accelerating.org/.

[2] R.E. Caves, 2000, p. 204.

[3] G. Mensch, 1979.

[4] E. Goldberg, 2005.

[5] C.S. Dodson et al., 1993; J.S. Schooler et al., 1993, both referred in M. Gladwell, 2005.

[6] H. Gedenryd, 1998.

[7] H. A. Simon, 1981.

[8] D. Schön, 1983.

[9] H. Petroski, 1995.

[10] Petroski, 1995.

[11] P. W. Swift, 1997.

[12] P. Schenk, 1991.

[13] C. Lorenz, 1986.

[14] Schenk, 1991.

[15] Schenk, 1991.

[16] O. Andersson, 1998.

[17] Andersson, 1998.

[18] R. H. McKim, 1980.

[19] M. Schrage, 2000, p. 83.

[20] Schenk, 1991.

[21] Schrage, 2000.

[22] McKim, 1980.

[23] T. Kelley, 2001.

[24] Miller, Arthur I. *Insights of Genius*. Cambridge, Massachusetts: MIT Press, 2000.

[25] Kelley, 2001, pp. 111–112.

[26] Schrage, 2000, p. 48.

[27] Schrage, 2000, p. 19.

[28] Schrage, 2000, pp. 72–74.

[29] A.B. Hargadon and R.I. Sutton, 2000, p. 157 ff.

[30] Hargadon and Sutton, 2000, p. 157 ff.

[31] Schrage, 2000, p. 64.

[32] Schrage, 2000, p. 14.

[33] A. B. Hargadon, 1998, p. 220.

[34] J. H. Holland, 1998.

[35] P. McCorduck, 1991.

[36] D. R. Hofstadter, 1985.

[37] Caves, 2000, p. 25.

# Appendix A

## INTERVIEW QUESTIONS FOR DESIGNERS AND DESIGN FIRMS

*1. General Issue — Role(s) (or Scope) of Design Firms*

How does the Design Firm conceive the diversity and scope of its resources and linking activities?

  a. Variety between firms — e.g., specialists vs. generalists

  b. Overlap with/difference from R&D firms/engineering consultancies

  c. Change over time — e.g., emergence of larger, multi-task firms (i.e., not just doing product design but also market research, communications strategy, etc. This relates to the longer term division of labor between design firms and their clients)

*2. The Client Interface (i.e., what is provided?)*

  a. Do design firms play the role of gatekeeper/broker — what does this role entail? (e.g., advice *not* to go ahead with new product development?)

  b. Nature of the relationship — relations with a few clients vs. jobbing with an ever-changing set of clients? (How often) Do client firms employ more than one design firm for the same project?

  c. Role as bridges between functions/departments within the client firm (or between clients and their suppliers)

d. How diverse are the client firms? Do design firms seek diverse client firms?

e. Does the design firm think about (and attempt to manage) its client portfolio?

f. What form(s) of output is/are expected/or available (i.e., where the design firm may set its boundaries) — concepts, drawings, prototypes, etc.?

g. Transcending the brief — how often is this done? Is it widely expected? Is it rewarded?

h. Clientless projects — do design firms develop product concepts without a client which they later try to sell/license to clients/producers?

i. Wider integration/coordination role

- Are design firms asked to do this/Do design firms see themselves as linking to the customers as well as the client?

- Building networks or teams of consultants beyond the design firm for a specific project (i.e., where additional competencies are required — moving towards the virtual firm)

j. Issues relating to the rewards from the activities and ownership of intellectual property

*3. Processes — (Project-oriented) Techniques and Tools for Developing (Product) Concepts*

Unpacking the process to get beyond the distinction between tacit and explicit knowledge. How does the design firm generate alternatives and variety (of solutions) including avoiding becoming locked in too early to one solution? How are preconceived or "tired" solutions avoided or minimized? How sophisticated and/or "broad-ranging" are the tools (i.e., going beyond the product object itself, to its wider presentation and/or promotion and/or function)?

Role of (in evoking or representing knowledge)

a. Text ("the brief") and numbers (e.g., technical specifications/ parameters)

b. Search tools and metrics (e.g., scorecard)

c. Techniques — e.g., roles of metaphor, analogy, playing devil's advocate, quality function deployment (QFD)

d. Informal interaction

e. Formal meeting/arrangement(s) — e.g., assigned liaison people

f. (Temporary) Project teams with people from different backgrounds

g. Internal venture teams

h. Focus groups/Joint problem solving sessions (with customers, but also potentially others — e.g., technologists)

i. Sketches & visualization

j. Information technology tools — e.g., computer aided design

k. Physical artefacts (e.g., evaluating/reverse engineering existing products)

l. Prototypes (and experimental development):

   • How many prototypes are typically developed for a project?

   • How are they generated?

   • How are they evaluated?

*4. Conflict Resolution/How is Synthesis or "Wholeness" Created?*

  a. How are conflicts resolved in design projects — e.g., between aesthetics, usability, cost, etc.?

  b. Issues concerning product architectures/platforms/families/ functional ecology/idealized or composite design — i.e., how the subsystems, and interfaces are conceived and defined)

*5. Process Development*

  a. How are the existing techniques assessed for inadequacies?

  b. How are new techniques identified, developed and integrated?

*6. Broader Learning*

How the firm develops its broader capabilities and integrate these with those external to the firm? Includes how the design firm views and learns about emerging technologies and concepts, and if it felt necessary stays close to cutting edge research?

  a. Hiring practices and sources (e.g., is the longer-term diversity of the team deliberately sought, or are people recruited for specific and immediate tasks?)

  b. Brokering between clients and communities (of practice)

  c. Rotation programmes/secondments, etc.

  d. Combination and recombination of ideas

  e. Visits (including to research establishments), conferences, placements in companies/groups

  f. Inter-project learning

   • Learning from successes and disappointments (Project evaluations)

   • Transferring knowledge between projects

  g. Mechanisms used to retain key personnel?

# Appendix B

## *FROM SKETCH TO PRODUCT*[1]

The following sequence of exhibits illustrates the process some designers employ, from sketching through to models and prototypes, and then the use of Computer-Aided Design (CAD) software.

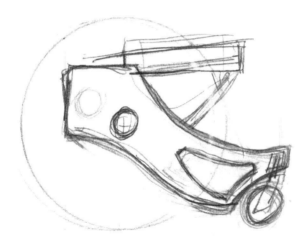

In the earliest stage, rough sketches like the one above concentrate on the essentials of whatever is being designed, while allowing for a concrete discussion with variations tried and tested. The industrial designer can then play around with the critical elements of the product idea, as in the next sketch.

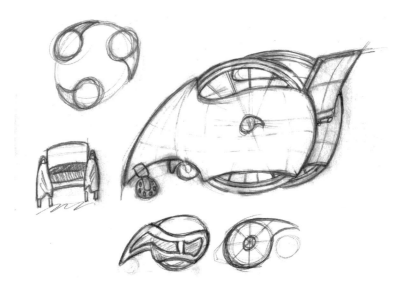

As the ideas converge towards agreement on the essentials, sketches grow increasingly distinct.

At this point in the process, measures, components, and systems are introduced — or at least they are hinted at, as in the next sketches.

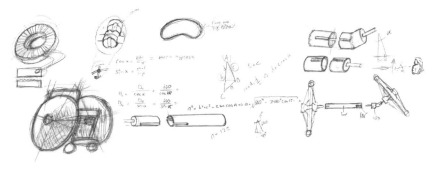

Often, the next step is to produce a mock-up, which may be made of clay, styrofoam, or any readily available and easily manipulated material. For this particular wheelchair design, the mock-up is cardboard. Designers may also take existing items to create a bricolage of whatever widgets are available that might "replicate" the design. This allows the designers to

test certain aspects of usability. Examples of both approaches are shown in the next photograph.

At some stage, sketches are upgraded to detailed drawings by hand, which in turn allow for renderings using CAD software.

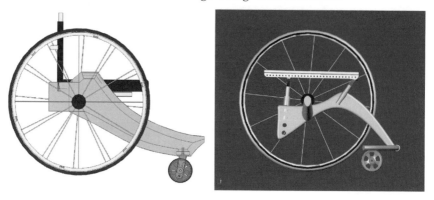

Rendering the details constitutes the basis for assembling the entire product or system within the computer, using the CAD software. CAD renderings also allow a means by which to highlight distinct features of the design.

CAD programs even allow for displaying the product as if it were real, employing lighting effects such as shadows, for instance — as in the next image.

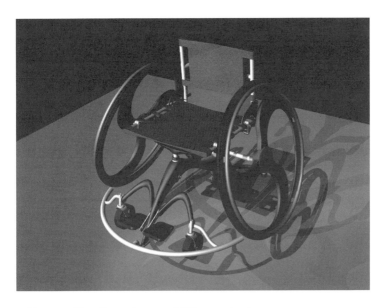

Eventually, there is a real-life product.

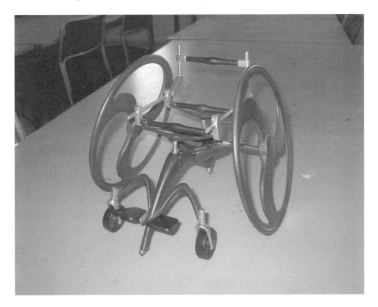

**Endnote**

---

[1]Our thanks to Marcus Seppälä for the material on wheelchairs.

# BIBLIOGRAPHY

Abernathy, W.J. and J.M. Utterback (1978). "Patterns of Industrial Innovation," *Technology Review*, Vol. 80, No. 7, June/July, 40–47.

Abernathy, W.J. and K.B. Clark (1985). "Innovation: Mapping the Winds of Creative Destruction," *Research Policy*, Vol. 14, No. 1, January, 3–22.

Ackoff, R. (1981). *Creating the Corporate Future*. New York: John Wiley & Sons.

Akrich, M. (1995). "User Representations: Practices, Methods and Sociology," in A. Rip, T.J. Misa, and J. Schot (eds.), *Managing Technology in Society: The Approach of Constructive Technology Assessment*, pp. 167–184. London and New York: Pinter Publishers.

Allen, T.J. (1977). *Managing the Flow of Technology*. Cambridge, MA: MIT Press.

Almeida, P. and B. Kogut (1999). "Localization of Knowledge and the Mobility of Engineers in Regional Networks," *Management Science*, Vol. 45, No. 7, July, 905–917.

Alvarez, E. (2000). "Identifying and Managing Sources of Creativity for Effective Product Innovation," Master of Science in Management of Technology Thesis, Massachusetts Institute of Technology, May.

Anderson, P. and M.L. Tushman (1990). "Technological Discontinuities and Dominant Designs: A Cyclical Model of Technological Change," *Administrative Science Quarterly*, Vol. 35, No. 4, December, 604–633.

Andersson, O. (1998). "The Searching Sketch," Lecture at the APSDA Conference, Malaysia.

Bertola, P. and J.C. Texeira (2003). "Design as a Knowledge Agent. How Design as a Knowledge Process is Embedded into Organizations to Foster Innovation," *Design Studies*, Vol. 24, No. 2, 181–194.

Bertola, P., S. Daniela, and S. Giuliano (2002). *Milano distretto del design — Un sistema di luoghi, attori e relazioni al servizio dell'innovazione*. Milano: Il Sole 24 Ore.

Bhat, S. and S.K. Reddy (1998). "Symbolic and Functional Positioning of Brands," *Journal of Consumer Marketing*, Vol. 15, No. 1, 32–47.

Bijker, W. and J. Law (eds.) (1994). *Shaping Technology/Building Society: Studies in Socio-Technical Change*. Cambridge, MA: MIT Press.

239

Bohn, R.E. (1994). "Measuring and Managing Technical Knowledge," *Sloan Management Review*, Vol. 36, No. 1, 61–73.

Borja de Mozota, B. (2003). *Design Management*. New York: Allworth Press.

Brown, S. (1995). *Postmodern Marketing*. London: Routledge.

Buchner, D. (2003). "The Role of Meaning and Intent," *Innovation*, Vol. 22, No. 1, 16–18.

BusinessWeek Online (2005). "Google's search for simplicity," 3 October.

Callon, M. (1991). "Techno-Economic Networks and Irreversibility," in J. Law (ed.), *A Sociology of Monsters: Essays on Power, Technology and Domination*, pp. 132–161. London: Routledge.

Canina, L., C.A. Enz, and J.S. Harrison (2005). "Agglomeration Effects and Strategic Orientations: Evidence from the U.S. Lodging Industry," *Academy of Management Journal*, Vol. 48, No. 4, August, 565–581.

Carlile, P.R. (2002). "A Pragmatic View of Knowledge and Boundaries: Boundary Objects in New Product Development," *Organization Science*, Vol. 13, No. 4, 442–455.

Caves, R.E. (2000). *Creative Industries*. Cambridge, MA: Harvard University Press.

Chesbrough, H.W. (2003). *Open Innovation: The New Imperative for Creating and Profiting from Technology*. Boston, MA: Harvard Business School Press.

Christensen, C.M. (1997). *The Innovator's Dilemma: When New Technologies Cause Great Firms to Fail*. Boston, MA: Harvard Business School Press.

Clark, K. and T. Fujimoto (1991). *Product Development Performance*. Boston, MA: Harvard Business School Press.

Conner K.R. and C.K. Prahalad (1996). "A Resource-Based Theory of the Firm: Knowledge Versus Opportunism," *Organization Science*, Vol. 7, No. 5, 477–501.

Conran, T. (1996). *Terence Conran on Design*. New York: Overlook Press.

Coombs, R., M. Harvey, and B.S. Tether (2003). "Analysing Distributed Processes of Provision and Innovation," *Industrial and Corporate Change*, Vol. 12, No. 6, 1125–1155.

Cooper, R.A. (1998). *Wheelchair Selection and Configuration*. New York: Demos Medical Publishing.

Cooper, R.A. (2001). "Improvements in Mobility for People with Disabilities." *Medical Engineering and Physics*, Vol. 23, No. 10, December, p. v.

Cooper, R.A. and M. Press (1995). *The Design Agenda*. Chichester, UK: John Wiley & Sons.

Cooper, R.A. *et al.* (2003). "Technical Perspectives. Use of the Independence 3000 IBOT Transporter at home and in the community," *Journal of Spinal Cord Medicine*, Vol. 26, 79–85.

Cross, N. (1995). "Discovering Design Ability," in R. Buchanan and V. Margolin (eds.), *Discovering Design – Explorations in Design Studies*, pp. 105–120. Chicago: University of Chicago Press.

Csikszentmihalyi, M. (2003). *Good Business: Leadership, Flow and the Making of Meaning*. New York: Hodder & Stoughton.

Csikszentmihalyi, M. and E. Rochberg-Halton (1981). *The Meaning of Things: Domestic Symbols and the Self*. Cambridge, UK: Cambridge University Press.

Cusumano, M., Y. Mylonadis, and R. Rosenbloom (1992). "Strategic Manuevering and Mass Market Dynamics: The Triumph of VHS over Beta," *Business History Review*, Vol. 66, Spring, 51–94.

Datson, T. (2003). "Google's Simplicity Earns Brand of the Year Honors," *Reuters*, 12 February.

Davenport, T.H. and L. Prusak (1998). *Working Knowledge: How Organizations Manage What They Know*. Boston, MA: Harvard Business School Press.

De Mozota, B.B. (2004). *Design Management*. Watson-Guptill.

De Rond, M. (2003). *Strategic Alliances as Social Facts*. Cambridge, UK: Cambridge University Press.

Design Council (1992). *British Design Awards Booklet*. London: The Design Council.

Dodgson, M., D. Gann, and A. Salter (2005). *Think, Play, Do: Technology, Innovation, and Organization*. Oxford, UK: Oxford University Press.

Dodson, C.S. *et al.* (1993). "The Verbal Overshadowing Effect: Why Descriptions Impair Face Recognition," *Memory & Cognition*, Vol. 25, No. 2, 129–139.

Dosi, G. (1982). "Technological Paradigms and Technological Trajectories," *Research Policy*, Vol. 11, No. 3, 147–162.

Drucker, P.F. (1985). "The Discipline of Innovation," *Harvard Business Review*, Vol. 63, No. 3, May–June, 67–72.

Durgee, J. and R.W. Veryzer (1999). *Products That Have Soul: Design Research Implications of Thomas Moore's "Re-Enchantment of Everyday Life"*. Rensselaer Polytechnic Institute.

Ellison, G. and E.L. Glaeser (1999). "The Geographic Concentration of Industry: Does Natural Advantage Explain Agglomeration?" *The American Economic Review*, Vol. 89, No. 2, May, 311–316.

Fischer, E. (2000). "Consuming Contemporaneous Discourses: A Postmodern Analysis of Food Advertisements Targeted Toward Women," *Advances in Consumer Research*, Vol. 27, No. 1, 288–294.

Fournier, S. (1991). "Meaning-Based Framework for the Study of Consumer/Object Relations," *Advances in Consumer Research*, Vol. 18, No. 1, 736–742.

Freeman, C. (1992). "Design and British Economic Performance," Lecture given at the Design Centre, London, 23 March. Quoted in Walsh *et al.* (1992).

Gedenryd, H. (1998). *How Designers Work*. Lund, Sweden: Lund University Cognitive Studies 75.

Geels, F.W. (2004). "From Sectoral Systems of Innovation to Socio-Technical Systems: Insights About Dynamics and Change from Sociology and Institutional Theory," *Research Policy*, Vol. 33, 897–920.

Gladwell, M. (2005). *Blink*. New York: Little Brown and Company.

Goldberg, E. (2005). *The Wisdom Paradox: How Your Mind Can Grow Stronger as Your Brain Grows Older*. New York: Gotham Books, as noted by Sue Halpern in *The New York Review of Books*, 28 April, pp. 19–21.

Gomory, R. (1983). "Technology Development," *Science*, Vol. 220, No. 4597, 576–580.

Gorb, P. and A. Dumas (1987). "Silent Design," *Design Studies*, Vol. 8, No. 3, 150–156.

Gotzsch, J. (2000). "Beautiful and Meaningful Products," Paper presented at the Politecnico di Milano Conference, *Design Plus Research*, 18–20, May.

Gotzsch, J. (2002). "Product Charisma," Paper presented at the Common Ground Conference at the Design Research Society at Brunel University, London, 5–7, September.

Grant, P.L. (2000). "Outsourced Knowledge: Knowledge Transfer and Strategic Implications from Design Outsourcing," Master of Science in Management of Technology Thesis, Massachusetts Institute of Technology, May.

Hargadon, A. (2003). *How Breakthroughs Happen: The Surprising Truth About How Companies Innovate*. Boston, MA: Harvard Business School Press.

Hargadon, A.B. and R.I. Sutton (1997). "Technology Brokering and Innovation in a Product Development Firm," *Administrative Science Quarterly*, Vol. 42, No. 4, December, 716–749.

Hargadon, A.B. and R.I. Sutton (2000). "Building an Innovation Factory," *Harvard Business Review*, Vol. 78, No. 3, May/June, 157–166.

Hargadon, A.B (1998). "Firms as Knowledge Brokers," *California Management Review*, Vol. 40, No. 3, Spring, 209–227.

Harrison, B., M.R. Kelley, and J. Gant (1996). "Innovative Firm Behavior and Local Milieu: Exploring the Intersection of Agglomeration, Firm Effects, and Technological Change," *Economic Geography*, Vol. 72, No. 3, July, 233–258.

Henderson, R.M. and K.B. Clark (1990). "Architectural Innovation: The Reconfiguration of Existing Product Technologies and the Failure of Established Firms," *Administrative Science Quarterly*, Vol. 35, No. 1, 9–30.

Hofstadter, D.R. (1985). *Metamagical Themas: Questing for the Essence of Mind and Pattern*. New York: Basic Books.

Holland, J.H. (1998). *Emergence*. Reading, MA: Helix Books.

Holt, D. (1997). "A Poststructuralist Lifestyle Analysis: Conceptualizing the Social Patterning of Consumption in Post-modernity," *Journal of Consumer Research*, Vol. 23, No. 4, March, 326–350.

Holt, D. (2003). "What Becomes an Icon Most?" *Harvard Business Review*, Vol. 81, No. 3, March, 43–49.

Howells, J. (1999). "Research and Technology Outsourcing," *Technology Analysis and Strategic Management*, Vol. 11, No. 1, 17–29.

Huston, L. and N. Sakkab (2006). "Connect and Develop: Inside Proctor & Gamble's New Model for Innovation," *Harvard Business Review*, Vol. 84, No. 3, March, 58–66.

Iansiti, M. (1998). *Technology Integration: Making Critical Choices in a Dynamic World*. Boston, MA: Harvard Business School Press.

Iansiti, M. and R. Levien (2004). *The Keystone Advantage: What the New Dynamics of Business Ecosystems Mean for Strategy, Innovation and Sustainability*. Boston, MA: Harvard Business School Press.

(The) Independent Guide to the 2004 Paralympics Games from Athens. http://www.paralympics.com.

(The) International Paralympic Committee. http://www.paralympic.org.

Johansson, F. (2004). *The Medici Effect: Breakthrough Ideas at the Intersection of Ideas, Concepts and Cultures*. Boston, MA: Harvard Business School Press.

Karjalainen, T.-M. (2003). "Strategic Design Language: Transforming Brand Identity into Product Design Elements," *10th EIASM International Product Development Management Conference*, Brussels, 10–11 June.

Kelley, T. (2001). *The Art of Innovation*. New York: Doubleday.

Kim, L. and J.M. Utterback (1983). "The Evolution of Organizational Structure and Technology in a Developing Country," *Management Science*, Vol. 29, No. 10, October, 1185–1197.

Kleine III, R.E., S.S. Kleine, and J.B. Kernan (1993). "Mundane Consumption and the Self: A Social-Identity Perspective," *Journal of Consumer Psychology*, Vol. 2, No. 3, 209–235.

Klevorik, A.K., R.C. Levin, R.R. Nelson, and S.G. Winter (1995). "On the Sources and Significance of Interindustry Differences in Technological Opportunties," *Research Policy*, Vol. 24, No. 2, March, 185–205.

Kogut, B. and U. Zander (1992). "Knowledge of the Firm: Combinative Capabilities and the Replication of Technology," *Organization Science*, Vol. 3, No. 3, 383–397.

Krippendorff, K. (1989). "On the Essential Contexts of Artifacts, or on the Proposition that 'Design is Making Sense (of Things),'" *Design Issues*, Vol. 5, No. 2, Spring, 9–38.

Kumar, V. and P. Whitney (2003). "Faster, Deeper User Research," *Design Management Journal*, Vol. 14, No. 2, Spring, 50–55.

Kurzweil, R. (2005). "Human 2.0," *New Scientist*, Vol. 187, No. 2518, 24–30 September, 32–36.

Lane, P. and M. Lubatkin (1998). "Relative Absorptive Capacity and Inter-Organizational Learning," *Strategic Management Journal*, Vol. 19, No. 5, May, 461–477.

Latour, B. (1987). *Science in Action: How to Follow Scientists and Engineers Through Society*. Cambridge, MA: Harvard University Press.

LEGO Mindstorms Robotics Invention System 2.0 Software. http://mindstorms.lego.com/eng/products/ris/rissoft.asp.

Lehnerd, A. (1987). "Revitalizing the Manufacture and Design of Mature Global Products," in B.R. Guile and H. Brooks, *Technology and Global Industry: Companies and Nations in the World Economy*, Series on Technology and Social Priorities, pp. 49–64. Washington, DC: National Academy of Engineering.

Leonard, D. (1998). *Wellsprings of knowledge: Building and Sustaining the sources of Innovation*. Boston, MA: Harvard Business School Press.

Levitt, T. (1986). *The Marketing Imagination*. New York: Free Press.

Lojacono, G. and G. Zaccai (2004). "The Evolution of the Design-Inspired Enterprise," *Sloan Management Review*, Vol. 45, No. 3, Spring, 75–79.

Lorenz, C. (1986). *The Design Dimension*. Oxford, UK: Blackwell (Revised 1990).

Maidique, M.A. and B.J. Zirger (1985). "The New Product Learning Cycle," *Research Policy*, Vol. 14, No. 6, December, 299–313.

Maldonado, T. (1964). *The Education of Industrial Designers*. UNESCO Seminar Report, Bruges, Belgium.

Malecki, E.J. (1985). "Industrial Location and Corporate Organization in High Technology Industries," *Economic Geography*, Vol. 61, No. 4, October, 345–369.

Mano, H. and R.L. Oliver (1993). "Assessing the Dimensionality and Structure of the Consumption Experience: Evaluation, Feeling, and Satisfaction," *Journal of Consumer Research*, Vol. 20, No. 3, 451–466.

Mansfield, H. (2000). *The Same Ax Twice: Restoration and Renewal in a Throwaway Age*. Hanover, NH: University Press of New England.

Margolin, V. and R. Buchanen (eds.) (1995). *The Idea of Design: A Design Issues Reader*. Cambridge, MA: MIT Press.

Maslow, A.H. (1998). *Maslow on Management*. New York: John Wiley & Sons.

McAlhone, B. (1987). *British Design Consultancy: Anatomy of a Billion Pound Business*. London: Design Council.

McCorduck, P. (1991). *Aaron's Code*. New York: W.H. Freeman and Company.

McKim, R.H. (1980). *Thinking Visually*. Belmont, CA: Lifetime Learning Publications.

Mensch, G. (1979). *Stalemate in Technology*. Cambridge, MA: Ballinger.

Meyer, M.H. and A.P. Lehnerd. (1997). *The Power of Product Platforms: Building Value and Cost Leadership*. New York: Free Press.

Meyer, M.H., P. Tertzakian and J.M. Utterback (1997). "Metrics for Managing Product Development," *Management Science*, Vol. 43, No. 1, January, 88–111.

Miller, A.I. (2000). *Insights of Genius*. Cambridge, MA: MIT Press.

Miller, R.E. and D. Sawers (1970). *The Technical Development of Modern Aviation*. New York: Praeger Publishers.

Mollerup, P. (1986). *Design for Life*. Copenhagen: Danish Design Council.

Moody, S. (1980). "The Role of Industrial Design in Technological Innovation," *Design Studies*, Vol. 1, No. 6, 329–339.

Moore, T. (1992). *Care of the Soul: A Guide for Cultivating Depth and Sacredness in Everyday Life*. New York: Harper Perennial.

Noehren, W.L. (1999). "Development and Empirical Investigation of a Boundary Object Richness Scale for Product Development Teams," Masters Thesis,

Alfred P. Sloan School of Management, Massachusetts Institute of Technology, June.

Norman, D.A. (2004). *Emotional Design: Why We Love (or Hate) Everyday Things*. New York: Basic Books.

Nussbaum, B. (2004). "The Power of Design," *Business Week*, 17 May.

OECD (1992). "Frascati Manual." http://www.oecd.org/pdf/M0000300/M00003664.pdf.

Oppenheimer, A. (2005). "Products Talking to People: Conversation Closes the Gap between Products and Consumers," *Journal of Product Innovation Management*, Vol. 22, No. 1, January, 82–91.

Papanek, V. (2004). *Design for the Real World: Human Ecology and Social Change*. London: Thames & Hudson (Reprinted 2004).

Pavitt, K. (2005). "Innovation Processes," in J. Fagerberg, D.C. Mowery, and R.R. Nelson (eds.), *The Oxford Handbook of Innovation*, pp. 86–114. Oxford, UK: Oxford University Press.

Peterson, R.A. and N. Anand (2004). "The Production of Culture Perspective," *Annual Review of Sociology*, Vol. 30, 311–334.

Petroski, H. (1995). *Engineers of Dreams*. New York: Alfred A Knopf.

Pham, M.T., J.B. Cohen, J.W. Pracejus, and G.D. Hughes (2001). "Affect Monitoring and the Primacy of Feelings in Judgment," *Journal of Consumer Research*, Vol. 28, No. 2, September, 167–188.

Phillips, A. (1971). *Technology and Market Structure: A Study of the Aircraft Industry*. Lexington, MA: Lexington Books.

Pinch, T. and W. Bijker (1987). "The Social Construction of Facts and Artifacts: Or How the Sociology of Science and the Sociology of Technology Might Benefit Each Other," in W. Bijker, T. Hughes, and T. Pinch (eds.), *The Social Construction of Technological Systems: New Directions in the Sociology and History of Technology*, pp. 17–50. Cambridge, MA: MIT Press.

Pine II, B.J. (1993). *Mass Customization*. Boston, MA: Harvard Business School Press.

Piore, M.J. and C.F. Sabel. (1984) *The Second Industrial Divide: Possibilities for Prosperity*. New York: Basic Books.

Porter, M. (1990). *The Competitive Advantage of Nations*. New York: Free Press.

Postrel, V. (2005). *The Substance of Style*. New York: Harper-Collins Publishers.

Pouder, R. and C.H. St. John (1996). "Hot Spots and Blind Spots: Geographical Clusters of Firms and Innovation," *The Academy of Management Review*, Vol. 21, No. 4, October, 1192–1225.

Powell, W.W. and S. Grodal (2005). "Networks of Innovators," in J. Fagerberg, D.C. Mowery and R.R. Nelson (eds.), *The Oxford Handbook of Innovation*, pp. 56–85. Oxford, UK: Oxford University Press.

Pugh, S. (1991). *Total Design: Integrated Methods for Successful Product Engineering*. Reading, MA: Addison Wesley.

Pulos, A.J. (1983). *American Design Ethic: A History of Industrial Design to 1940.* Cambridge, MA: MIT Press.

Reingold, J. (2005). "What P&G Knows About the Power of Design," *Fast Company*, Vol. 95, June, 56–57.

Rickne, A. (2000). "New Technology-based Firms and Industrial Dynamics: Evidence from the Technological System of Biomaterials in Sweden, Ohio and Massachusetts," Doctoral Dissertation, Department of Industrial Dynamics, Chalmers University of Technology, Göteborg, Sweden.

Rogers, E.M. (1995). *Diffusion of Innovations, 4th Ed.* New York: The Free Press.

Rothwell, R. (1986). "Innovation and Re-Innovation: A Role for the User," *Journal of Marketing Management*, Vol. 12, No. 2, 19–29.

Rust, R.T., D.V. Thompson, and R.W. Hamilton. (2006). "Defeating Feature Fatigue," *Harvard Business Review*. Vol. 84, No. 2, February, 98–107.

Sanderson, S. and V. Uzumeri (1997). *The New Competitive Edge: Managing Product Families.* Homewood, IL: Richard D. Irwin.

Schenk, P. (1991). "The Role of Drawing in the Graphic Design Process," *Design Studies*, Vol. 12, No. 3, July, 168–181.

Schmitt, B. (1999). *Experiential Marketing: How to Get Customers to Sense, Feel, Think, Act and Relate to Your Company and Brands.* New York: Free Press.

Schön, D. (1983). *The Reflective Practitioner.* Cambridge, MA: MIT Press.

Schooler, J.S. *et al.* (1993). "Thoughts Beyond Words: When Language Overshadows Insight," *Journal of Experimental Psychology*, Vol. 122, No. 2, 166–183.

Schrage, M. (2000). *Serious Play.* Boston MA: Harvard Business School Press.

Schwartz, E.I. (2002). "The Inventors Playground," *Technology Review*, Vol. 105, No. 8, October, 69–73.

Sentance, A. and J. Clark (1997). The Contribution of Design to the UK Economy — A Design Council Research Paper. London: Design Council.

Shah, S.K. (2005). "Open Beyond Software," in D. Cooper, C. Di Bona and M. Stone (eds.), *Open Sources 2*. Sebastopol, CA: O'Reilly Media.

Sherer, F.M. (1999). *New Perspectives on Economic Growth and Technological Innovation*, Brookings Institution Press, Washington, DC.

Sherman, E. (2002). "Inside the Apple iPOD Design Triumph," *Electronics Design Chain*, cover story, Summer 2002.

Simon, H.A. (1981). *The Sciences of the Artificial.* Cambridge, MA: MIT Press.

Skeens, N. and E. Farrelly (2000). *Future Present.* London: Booth-Clibborn Editions Ltd.

Sonn, U. and G. Grimby (1994). "Assistive Devices in an Elderly Population Studied at 70 and 76 Years of Age," *Disability and Rehabilitation*, Vol.16, No. 2, 85–93.

Sorenson, O. and D.M. Waguespack (2005). "Research on Social Networks and the Organization of Research and Development: An Introductory Essay," *Journal of Engineering and Technology Management*, Vol. 22, No. 1–2, March–June, 1–7.

(The) Swedish Federation for Disabled. DHR, http://www.dhr.se.

(The) Swedish Handicap Institute, http://www.hi.se.

Swift, P.W. (1997). "Science Drives Creativity: A Methodology for Quantifying Perceptions," *Design Management Journal*, Vol. 8, No. 2, Spring, 51–57.

Tsai, S.-P. (2005). "Utility, Cultural Symbolism and Emotion: A Comprehensive Model of Brand Purchase Value," *International Journal of Research in Marketing*, Vol. 22, No. 3, 277–291.

Tunisini, A. and A. Zanfei (1998). "Exploiting and Creating Knowledge Through Customer–Supplier Relationships: Lessons From a Case Study," *R&D Management*, Vol. 28, No. 2, 111–118.

Ulrich, K.T. and S.D. Eppinger (2004). *Product Design and Development*, $3^{rd}$ Ed. New York: McGraw-Hill.

Utterback, J.M. (1994). *Mastering The Dynamics of Innovation*. Boston MA: Harvard Business School Press.

Utterback, J.M. and A.N. Afuah (1998). "The Dynamic 'Diamond': A Technological Innovation Perspective," *Economics of Innovation and New Technology*, Vol. 2, No. 2, 3, June, 183–199.

Utterback, J.M. *et al.* (1988). "Technology and Industrial Innovation in Sweden: A study of Technology-based Firms Formed Between 1965 and 1980," *Research Policy*, Vol. 17, 15–26.

Utterback, J.M. and H.J. Acee (2005). "Disruptive Technologies: an Expanded View," *International Journal of Innovation Management*, Vol. 9, No. 1, March, 1–17.

Utterback, J.M. and W.J. Abernathy (1975). "A Dynamic Model of Product and Process Innovation," *Omega*, Vol. 3, No. 6, 639–656.

Verganti, R. (2003). "Design as Brokering of Languages: The Role of Designers in the Innovation Strategy of Italian Firms," *Design Management Journal*, Vol. 14, No. 3, Summer, 34–42.

Verganti, R. and C. Dell'Era (2003). *I Distretti del Design: Modello e Quadro Comparato delle Politiche di Sviluppo*. Milano: Report Finlombarda.

Verspagen, B. and C. Werker (2003). See http://tm-economics.tm.tue.nl/icol/icolrep.pdf.

Veryzer, R.W. and B.B. de Mozota (2005). "The Impact of User-Oriented Design on New Product Development: An Examination of Fundamental Relationships," *Journal of Product Innovation Management*, Vol. 22, No. 2, March, 128–143.

von Hippel, E. (1988). *Sources of Innovation*. New York: Oxford University Press.

von Hippel, E. (2005). *Democratizing Innovation*. Cambridge, MA: MIT Press.

von Hippel, E. *et al.* (1999). "Creating Breakthroughs at 3M," *Harvard Business Review*, Vol. 77, No. 5, 47–57.

Vredenburg, K., S. Isensee and C. Righi (2002). *User-Centered Design: An Integrated Approach*. Saddle River, NJ: Prentice-Hall.

Walsh, V. (1996). "Design, Innovation and the Boundaries of the Firm," *Research Policy*, Vol. 25, No. 4, June, 509–529.

Walsh, V., R. R.oy, M. Bruce, and S. Potter (1992). *Winning by Design: Technology, Product Design and International Competitiveness.* Oxford, UK: Blackwell Publishers.

Wernerfelt, B. (1984). "A Resource-Based View of the Firm," *Strategic Management Journal*, Vol. 5, No. 2, April, 171–180.

Yamaguchi, J.K., J. Thomson, and H. Tajima (1989). *Miata: Mazda MX–5.* St. Martins Press.

# NAME INDEX

**249**

Vedin, Bengt-Arne, ix, x
Verganti, Roberto, x, 156, 174, 203
Veryzer, Robert W., 203
VIGIX kiosk, 113
VIGIX logo, 114, 116
VIGIX, Inc., 112–116
Virgin Radio, 53
Volkswagen Beetle, 31, 53
Volvo Car Corporation, 52, 130, 131
von Hippel, Eric, 27, 105, 122, 170, 190

Walsh, Vivien, 60–63, 69
Welsh, Bob, 104
WGBH (Boston radio & public television station), 52
White Design industrial design group, 148
Wilbur, Tammy, 198

Wolfson Codec, 51
World Cup, 93
World War II, 34

Xerox copier, 29
Xerox PARC's Altos, 55

Yahoo! Inc., 15
Yale University, 32
Yamaguchi, Jack K., 34
Ytterborn & Fuentes (Y & F) design firm, 145, 146

Zaccai, Gianfranco, 88, 127, 184
Zanfei, Antonello, 119
Zippo lighter, 41
Zirger, Billie Jo, 27

# SUBJECT INDEX

257